post-hypnotic

ross bleckner steve di benedetto
judy ledgerwood stratton cherouny
mark dagley philip taaffe sarah morris
karin davie michelle grabner peter halley
jim isermann yayoi kusama tom martinelli
tom moody aaron parazette bruce pearson
peter schuyff walter robinson michael scott
jason martin james siena john armleder
susie rosmarin tad griffin fred tomaselli
david szafranski yek david clarkson

curated by barry blinderman

with essays by tom moody and
barry blinderman

university galleries
illinois state university
normal, illinois

post-hypnotic

This publication has been supported in part by grants from the National Endowment for the Arts and the Illinois Arts Council, a state agency.

Design: Bill Conger and Barry Blinderman
Production assistance: Matt Pulford and Karl Rademacher
Editorial assistance: C. K. Sample
Publisher: University Galleries of Illinois State University
Distributor: Distributed Art Publishers, New York
Printing: Bolger—Concept To Print, Minneapolis, Minnesota

Front cover detail: Mark Dagley, **Concentric Sequence**, 1996
Back cover detail: Susie Rosmarin, **Static Study #45**, 1998

exhibition itinerary:

January 12 - February 21, 1999
University Galleries, Normal, Illinois

June 12 - July 25, 1999
The McKinney Avenue Contemporary (The MAC), Dallas, Texas

September 4 - November 7, 1999
The Contemporary Arts Center, Cincinnati, Ohio

January 28 - March 12, 2000
Atlanta College of Art Gallery, Atlanta, Georgia

April 22 - June 25, 2000
Chicago Cultural Center, Chicago, Illinois

February 6 - April 8, 2001
Tweed Museum of Art, University of Minnesota, Duluth

University Galleries, Campus Box 5620, Normal, Illinois 61790
ph 309.438.5487 fax 438.5161; email: gallery@oratmail.cfa.ilstu.edu

ISBN 0-945558-29-5

NATIONAL ENDOWMENT FOR THE ARTS

Illinois ARTS Council
AN AGENCY OF THE STATE OF ILLINOIS

table of contents

the responsive mind

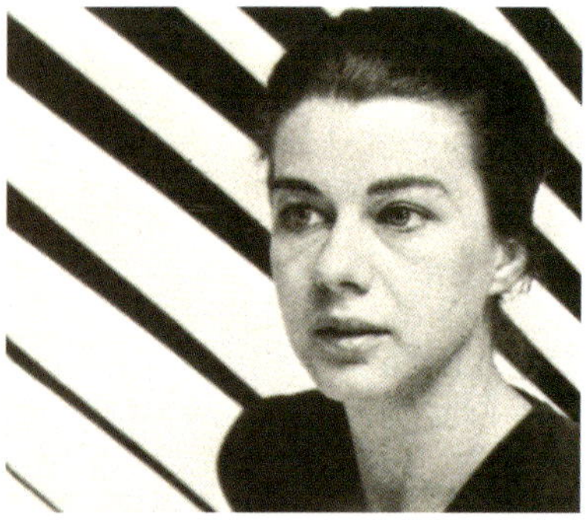

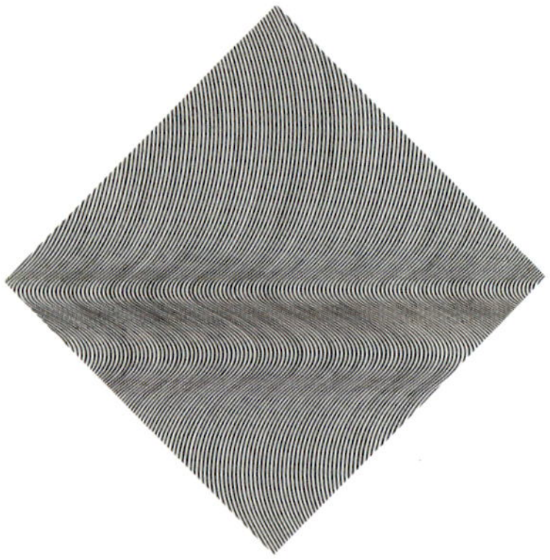

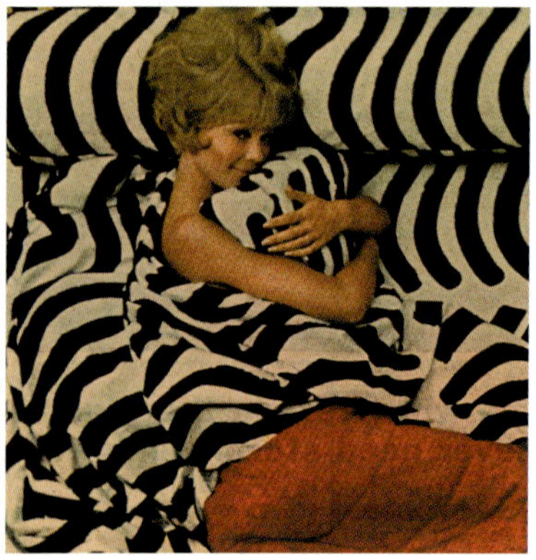

The message of any medium or technology is the change of scale or pace or pattern that it introduces into human affairs.
—Marshall McLuhan, *Understanding Media,* 1964

Peaking in the wake of mid-1960s World's Fair optimism, Op art lost its critical appeal as it shifted almost overnight from canvas into clothing design, poster art, and shopping mall supergraphics. Since the 1980s, however, numerous artists have revisited perceptual phenomena such as pulsating patterns, afterimages, vibrating illusionistic space, and other sensations often associated with altered states. post-hypnotic examines the resurgence of pronounced optical effects in the work of twenty-eight painters living in the U.S., Europe, and Japan. Although some of the paintings selected are isolated instances of Op in the work of artists for whom such concerns are secondary, my desire was to present enough examples of a tendency to argue that it is not an aberration, but a serious consideration among a wide range of artists.

The kind of vibratory, multifocal opticality addressed here is not the exclusive property of Bridget Riley, Victor Vasarely, Richard Anuskiewicz, and others specifically associated with Op—it is present also in work by Barnett Newman, Andy Warhol, Ellsworth Kelly, Sol LeWitt, Robert Indiana, and even in Jasper Johns' color-reversed Flags. In his artist roster for "The Responsive Eye" exhibition at MoMA in 1965—generally considered the alpha and omega of Op—curator William Seitz included Agnes Martin, Larry Bell, Morris Louis, Kenneth Noland, and Frank Stella, artists only peripherally engaged in what the curator termed "perceptual abstraction." A question Seitz asks in the concluding paragraph of his catalogue essay is quite telling of the conceptual difference between 60s perceptual abstraction and the work in post-hypnotic: “Can such works, that refer to nothing outside themselves, replace with psychic effectiveness the content that has been abandoned?”[1]

Although post-hypnotic is not intended primarily as a “deconstruction” of a past movement, as was characteristic in the 80s,[2] the work in the exhibition, referencing both post-war abstraction and aspects of daily life such as corporate architecture, TV commercials and cartoons, domestic furnishings, and computer-generated design, could hardly be considered contentless. In an age characterized by cultural amnesia, it tracks, in a critically informed way, the ever-accelerating transmutation of art into pop culture and back into art again. Heraclitus’ maxim—that one cannot bathe in the same river twice—is of particular relevance to anyone trying to figure out how (in our post-movement time) art of one period can really relate to that of another.

First of all, very few of the paintings shown here could have been conceived of in the 60s—the imprint of digital media and the culture’s full absorption of psychedelia, rock music, and television was still yet to come. But perhaps the more salient issue is that classic Op art no longer registers in our Cartoon Networked eyes and Y2K minds the way it did when it had its moment of glory at MoMA in 1965. It is sensibility which invests meaning in art, and sensibility changes like the waters in Heraclitus’ stream. New art is constantly altering the meaning of earlier art. As the recent Bridget Riley retrospective at the Serpentine Gallery in London demonstrates, Damien Hirst, Philip Taaffe, Peter Davies, and Karin Davie didn’t just respond to and recontextualize the work of the celebrated British Op artist, they recreated it in their own image.

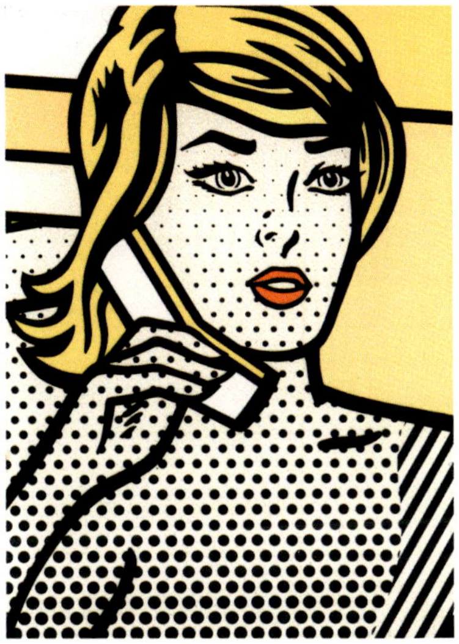

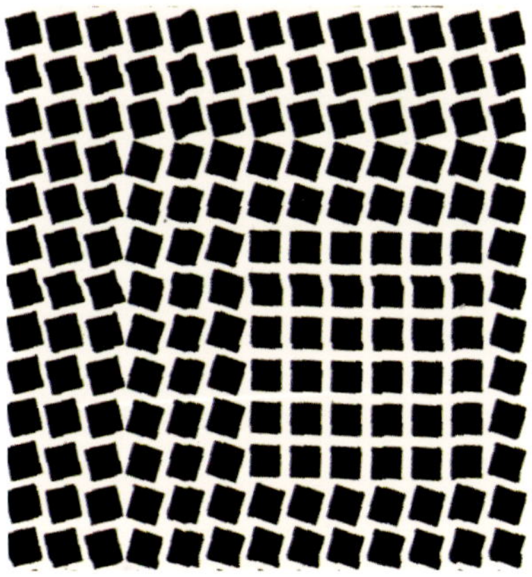

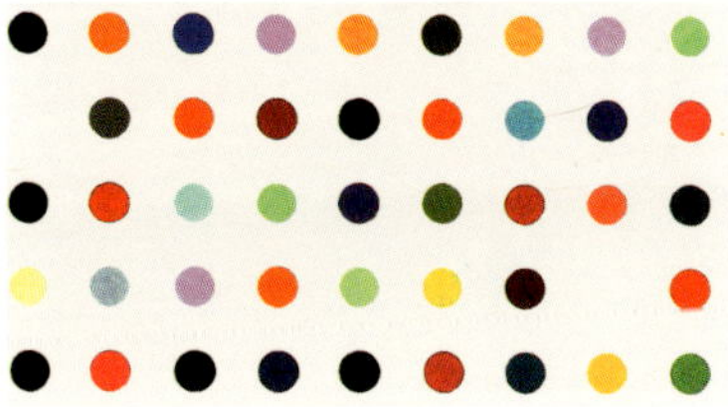

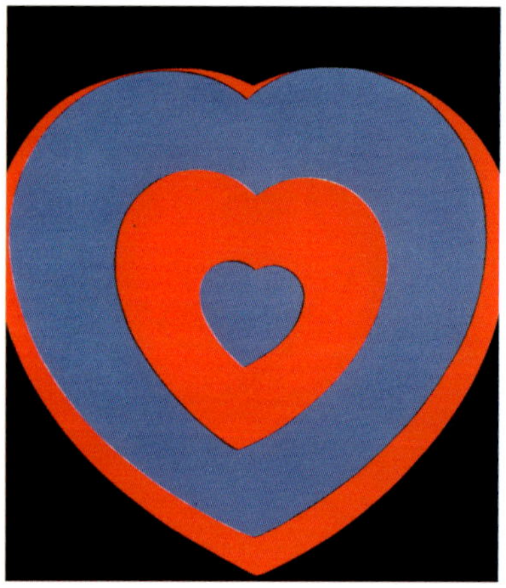

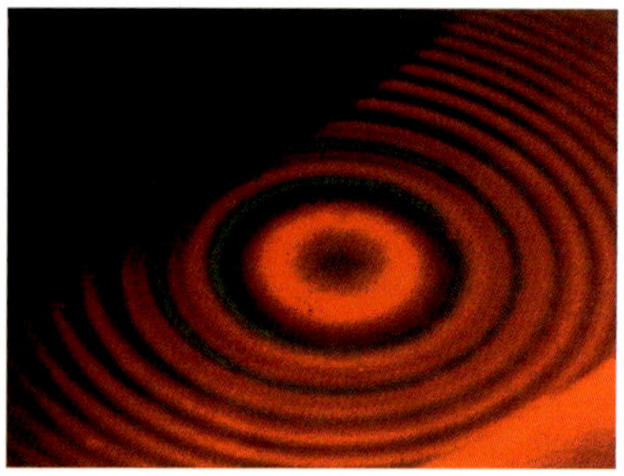

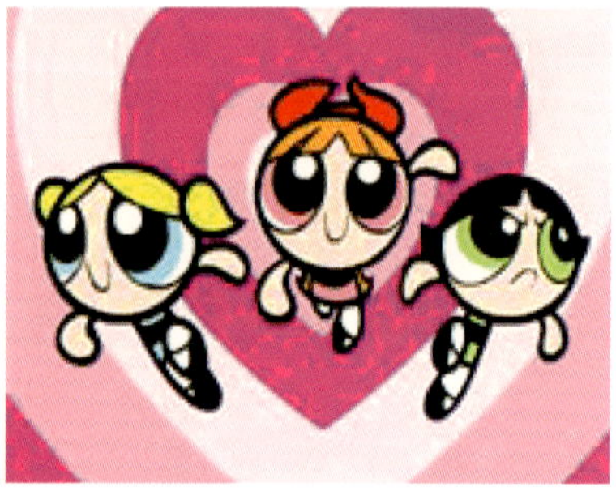

Whatever theory of evolution, death, resurrection, or reincarnation of painting you subscribe to, one thing is plain to anyone who bothers to take a close look: painting is trying to get out of itself, to spring into the more travelled zones of the semiotic spectrum. Ironically, one of the most intriguing ways in the 90s to accomplish this escape act is not, as in previous decades or in current installation-based art, to abandon the format of a two-dimensional rectangular support hung on a wall, but rather to subvert it while embracing it. In order to avoid the Euclidian confines of linear perspective and the equally limiting high modernist delusion of flatness, the artists in post-hypnotic choose to create a space situated neither through the canvas nor on its surface, but one that projects outward into the viewer's realm. This is screen-based thinking, practiced intuitively by the first two generations of image makers for whom television and computers are not mere inventions, but the tangible apparitions which convey experience. Responding to the mesmerizing patterns in their work that emerge like rainbows in pools of oil and water, we become conscious of a layer that removes itself from the support—exists outside of painting—despite the grounding references to modernist painting's heyday in the 1950s and 60s.

Variations in color, brightness, movement, perspective, symmetry, and replication provide finer gradation of the subjective experience. These are not just visual phenomena, but sensory form constants that are apparent in any spatially-extended sense. Initially, we thought these spatial configurations reflected some anatomic structure; then we tried mapping it to some prototypical function. Now, neuroscience is not sure what their physical correlates are, but many people do suspect that the form constants point to some deep, fundamental aspect of perception.

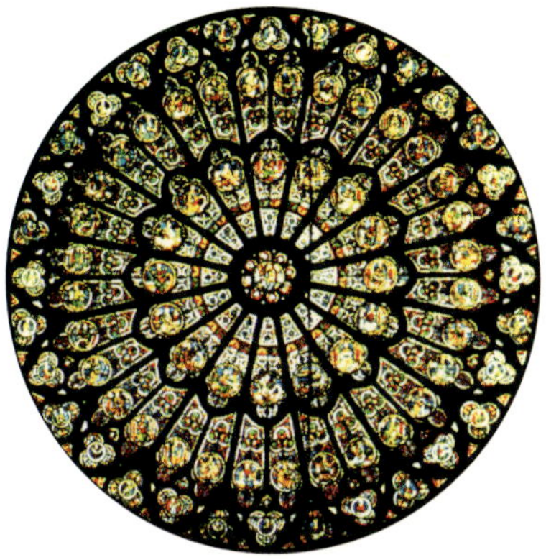

Synesthesia is projected. It is perceived externally in peri-personal space, the limb-axis space immediately surrounding the body, never at a distance as in the spatial teloreception of vision or audition. My subject DS, for example, . . . on hearing music, also sees objects—falling gold balls, shooting lines, metallic waves like oscilloscope tracings—that float on a "screen" six inches from her nose.

—Richard Cytowic, "Synesthesia: Phenomenology and Neuropsychology," *Psyche*, 2 (10), July 1995, 4.3, 7.3.

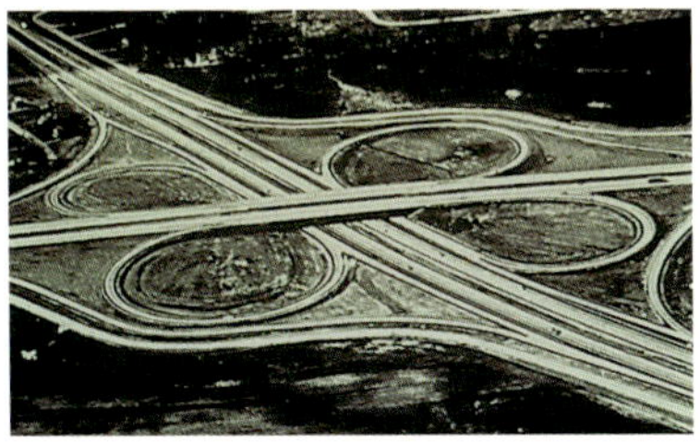

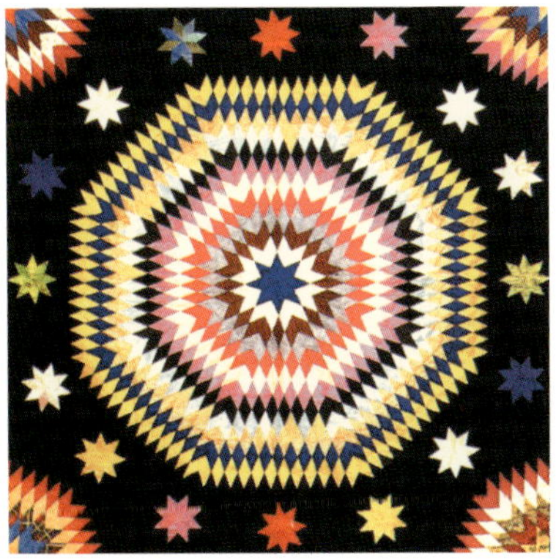

The above passages on synesthesia ("joined sensation"), the rare capacity to hear colors, see sounds, taste shapes or see certain letters as having individual colors, suggest a connection between the crossover of sight and sound occurring in this condition (which incidentally fascinated Kandinsky, the composer Scriabin, and other artists, poets, and musicians near the turn of the century[3] who were attempting a fusion of the arts) and the "external layer" of painting discussed in the preceding paragraph. As synesthesia is a projected phenomenon, so is our disorienting response to optical art—on extended viewing, patterns appear to float between the painting (especially those by Michael Scott, Tad Griffin, and Susie Rosmarin) and the viewer in a manner similar to Dr. Cytowic's subject's perception of a floating screen. Does our inability to focus on an image open a gateway to "phylogenetically older, subcortical brain structures involved in emotion and other primal functions"?[4] Neuroscientists' theories about "form constants" predating the separation of sensory pathways shed light on our powerful attraction to flickering lights, sensations of deep space, and repeated geometric patterning—phenomena exploited on a grand scale by the Catholic Church (stained glass, towering spires), city planners (grids of roadways with streetlights on every corner), domestic designers (wallpaper patterns, clothing and bedsheet design), and, of course, corporate advertising.

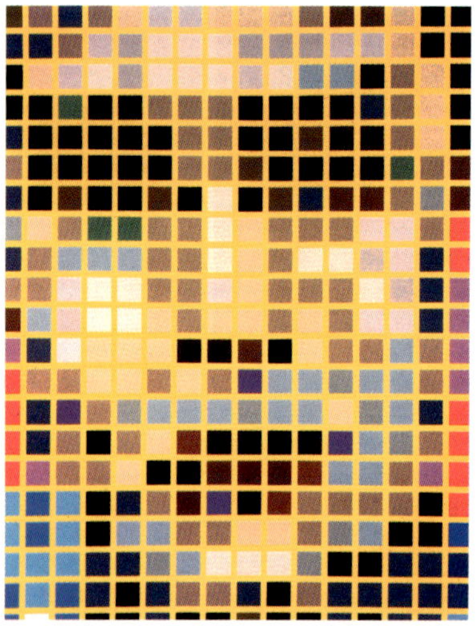

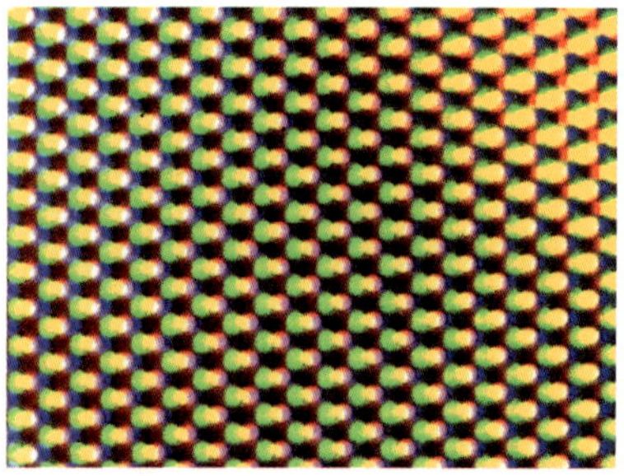

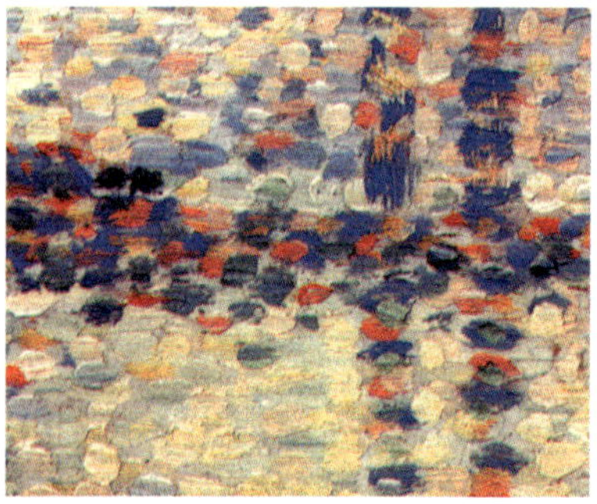

Painting's ability to project beyond itself argues for its continued relevance at the millennial crossroads—it is at once a sign of the hand, a surrogate for our corporeality, and a precursor to the virtual nexus of "graphical user interface." Yet unlike a digital file, in which every duplicate is an original, a painting is also a distinct mark in time, a marking of time. It is an experience by the artist of movement and additive process through time, which in turn unfolds before the viewer who encounters it at a later time. Painting is a pathway created through the registering of a trace, whether expressed in grid format (Halley, Griffin, Grabner, Morris, Scott, Schuyff, Rosmarin), in circular format (Dagley, Taaffe, Clarkson, Armleder, Robinson), or in combination (Moody, Bleckner, Ledgerwood, Siena). From the city grid to the internet, from the industrial to the post-digital, roads and electronic pathways have progressively decreased the amount of time it takes to get information from one place to another. Someone halfway around the world can hear a speaker's voice a fraction of a second earlier than a person sitting in the back of the lecture hall. Paradoxically, the artists in post-hypnotic slow down this passage of time, converting spatial elements—grids, circles, dots, or stripes—into temporal ones, measuring out sensation like the ticks of an atomic clock.

The TV image . . . exists by light through rather than by light on, and the image so formed has the quality of sculpture and icon, rather than of picture.

—McLuhan, op. cit.

We can posit a progression from Seurat's optical rebuilding of color from points of contrasting hue, coinciding with mid-nineteenth century color theories by Chevreul and Rood, to

Kandinsky's synesthetic correlation of tone, hue and pitch in music and art in his influential 1910 publication, Concerning the Spiritual in Art, to Duchamp's Rotoreliefs and Rotary Demispheres of the 1920s and 30s, rendering the third dimension visible through the rotation of irregular spirals on cardboard or glass, to Warhol's acrid color schemes and mass repetition of single images, closely anticipating the trancelike repeated cadences of rock music, to Op art, infusing formalist abstraction with Gestalt and other theories of perception, to Neo-Geo in the 80s, converting Op into high-gloss simulacra, and finally to the artists in this exhibition, reflecting on the overwhelming effect of the digital landscape. As alluded to above, however, both Op and screen-seeing really begin with stained glass windows in Gothic cathedrals—illuminated from outside, from behind, offering not the reflection of light, but light itself. These geometric arrangements of variously hued glass fragments are the true progenitors of pixels on a computer screen.

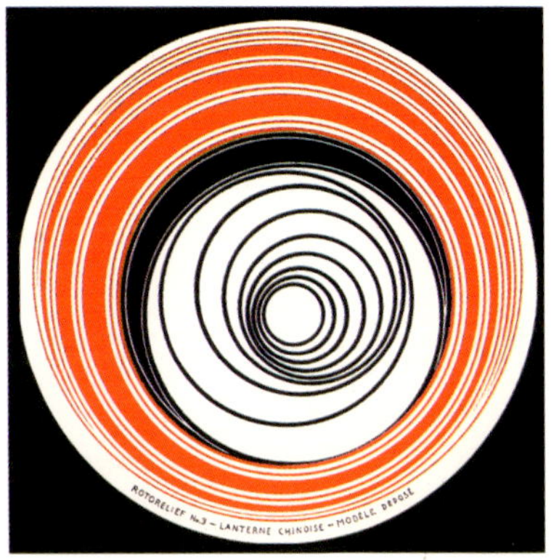

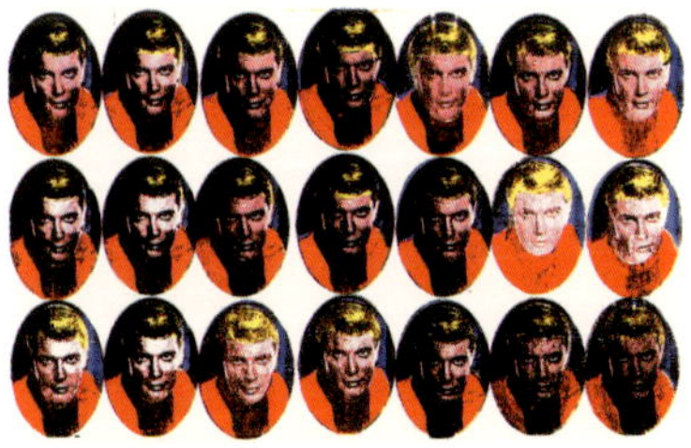

Op's burgeoning and diverse presence in the work of emerging artists suggests that it is an ongoing concern. The 80s emphasis on simulation and "faster paintings" has diminished in favor of the phenomenological, the temporal, and the experiential. A revived interest in modernist abstraction combines with far-reaching popular reference in paintings that may appear at first glance to be nothing more than patterned stripes, spots, concentric circles, or spirals. Investigating what Fred Tomaselli has called "the mechanics of seduction," the work in this exhibition links the "form constants" of inner experience, perceived spatially and temporally, with the increasingly complex structures of the everyday world.

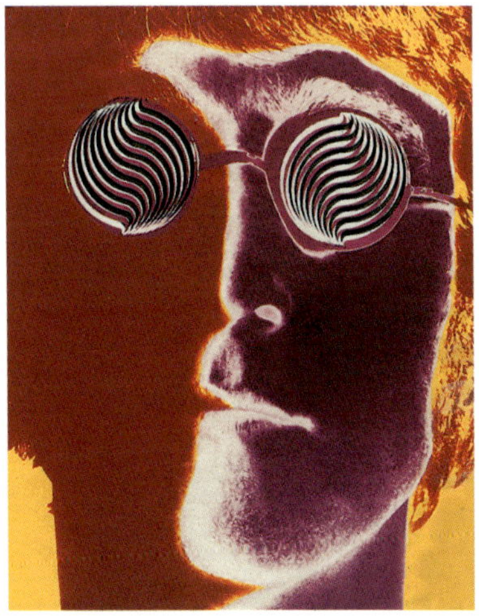

essay notes

[1] William Seitz, essay for *The Responsive Eye,* The Museum of Modern Art, New York, 1965, p.43.

[2] See Peter Halley, "Ross Bleckner: Painting at the End of History," *Arts,* May 1982, pp. 132-133, for a discussion on Bleckner's ironic appropriation of Op in his paintings.

[3] "The [20th century] composer Olivier Messiaen, speaking of the union of color and tone in his music, explained to an interviewer: 'When I hear music, I see inwardly, in the mind's eye, colors which move with the music. This is not imagination, nor is it psychic phenomenon. It is an inward reality.'" (Erica Goode, "When People See a Sound and Hear a Color," *The New York Times,* February 23, 1999).

[4] Erica Goode, op. cit.

essay photos

Page 4

Unattributed photograph of Bridget Riley c. 1964, John Russell, "Double Portrait: Phillip King and Bridget Riley," *Art in America,* May-June 1967, p. 98.

Bridget Riley, **Crest**, 1964, Emulsion on hardboard, 65 3/8 x 65 3/8 inches. The British Council.

Detail of a photograph by Tony Vaccaro, "Bright Spirit of Marimekko," *Life,* June 24, 1966, p. 69.

Page 5

Roy Lichtenstein, **Nude with Yellow Flower** (detail), 1994. Collection of Stephen T. Ellis. © Estate of Roy Lichtenstein.

Victor Vasarely, **Eridian-C no. 33** (detail), 1963, 25 x 28 inches. Denise René Gallery, Paris.

Damien Hirst, **Argininosuccinic Acid** (detail), 1995, Gloss household paint on canvas, 132 x 180 inches. Saatchi Gallery, London.

Page 6

Marcel Duchamp, **Fluttering Hearts** 1936, 13 x 20 inches. Gimpel Fils, London.

"Newton's Rings" (a series of concentric interference fringes), *The World Book Encyclopedia of Science, Vol. 2: Physics Today,* p. 89.

Power Puff Girls image, ™ Cartoon Network.

Page 7

The Rose Window north, c. 1250, Notre Dame Cathedral, built by Jean de Chelles, Paris.

Highway cloverleaf image from website of R.D. Walker VPI&SU, Transportation Research Board -11.

Detail of cover reproduction, Shelly Zebart, *American Quilt Collections,* 1997, Nihon Vogue Ltd. publishers.

Page 8

Sarah Morris, **STVNGNTRSK**, 1999, household gloss on canvas, 101 x 78 inches. Courtesy White Cube, London.

Close-up of a color television screen, *The World Book Encyclopedia of Science, Vol. 2: Physics Today,* p. 85.

George Seurat, **Study for Channel at Gravelines, Evening** (detail), 1890, oil on wood, 15 1/2 x 25 1/2 inches. Musée de l'Annonciade, Saint-Tropez.

Page 9

Marcel Duchamp, **Rotorelief No. 3: Lanterne Chinoise**, 1935.

Andy Warhol, **Troy Donohue** (detail), 1962, silkscreen ink and synthetic polymer paint on canvas, 80 3/4 x 60 inches. © 2000 Andy Warhol Foundation for the Visual Arts/ARS, New York.

John Lennon (detail) © Richard Avedon, 1967.

plates
artist profiles

john armleder

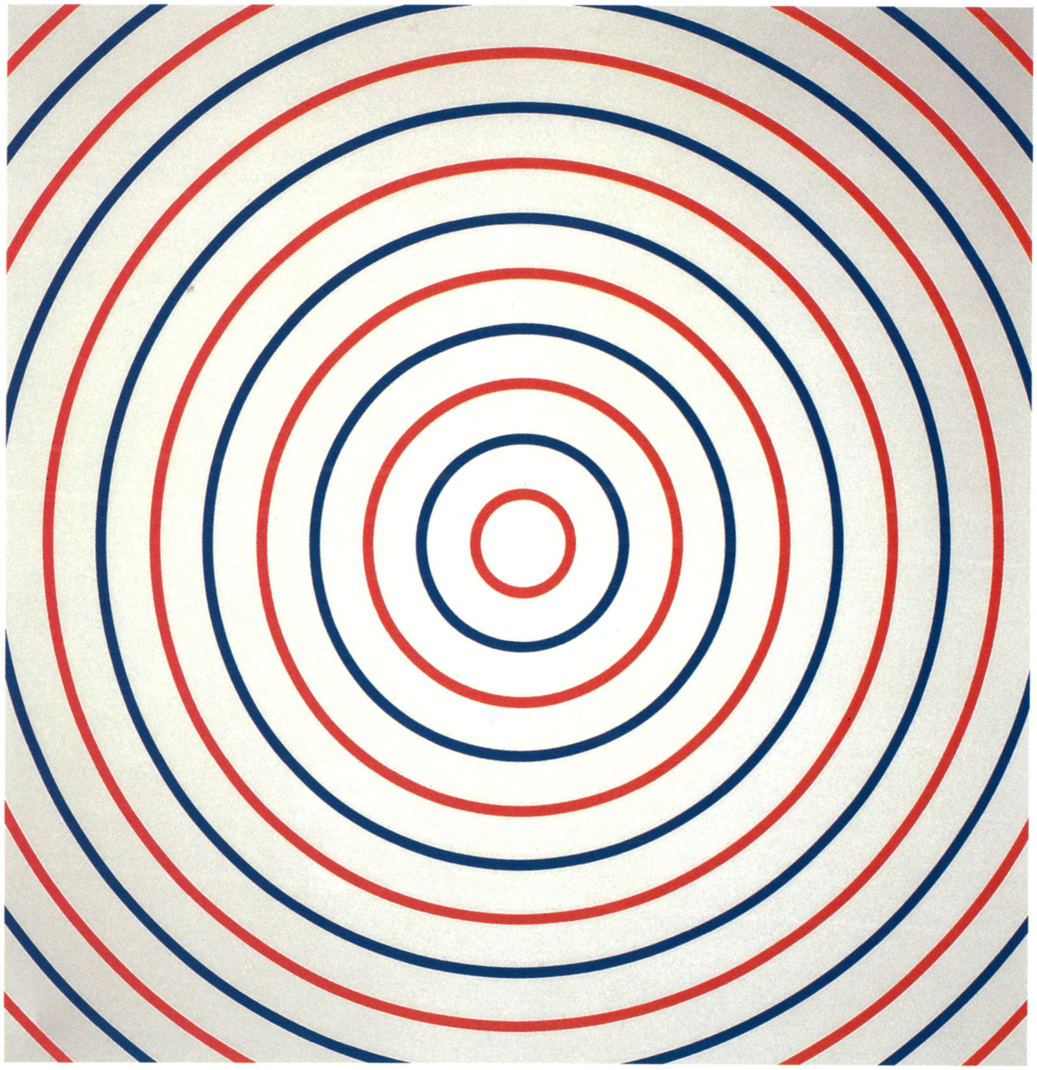

GOG Suite, 1996, silkscreen ink on paper, 19 5/8 x 19 5/8 inches

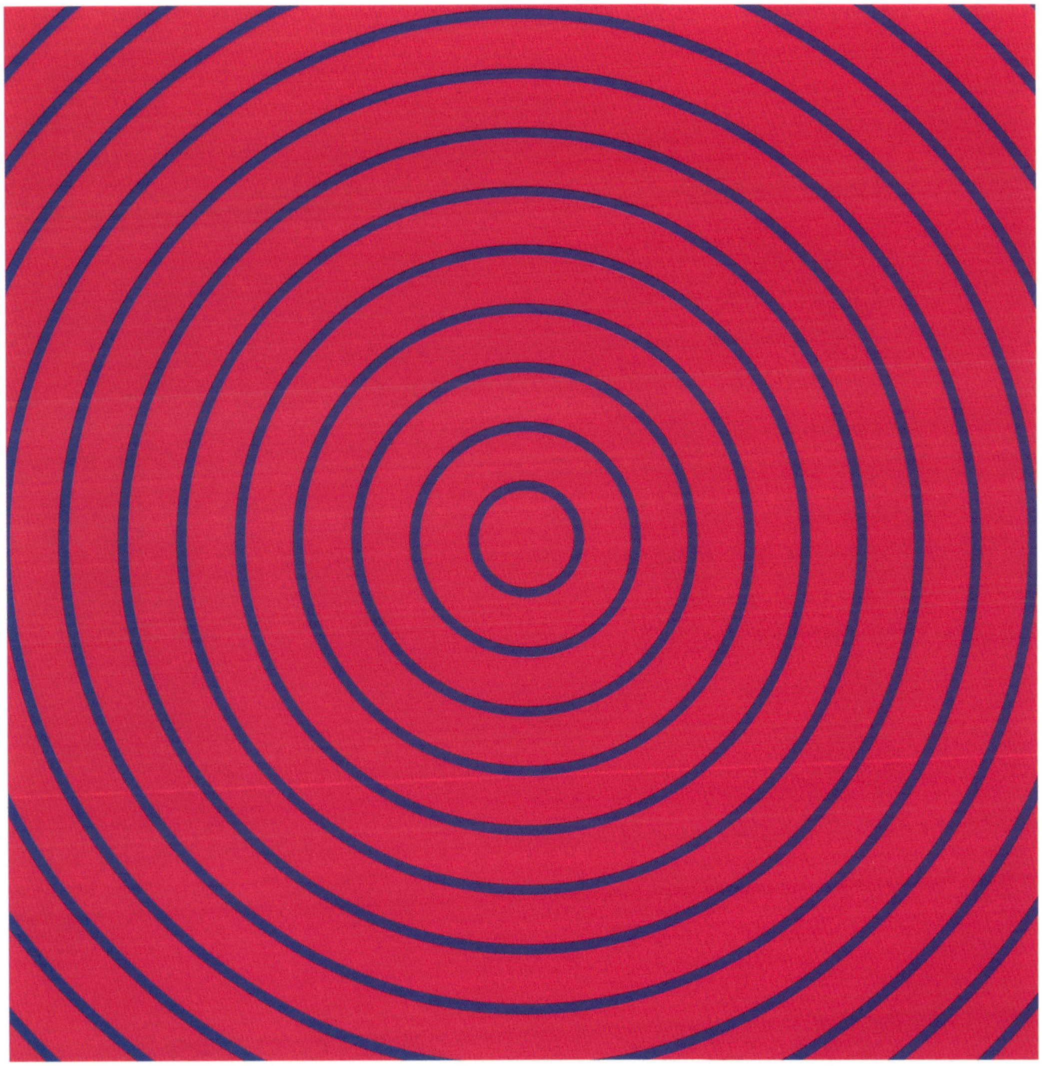

GOG Suite, 1996, silkscreen ink on paper, 19 5/8 x 19 5/8 inches

born: 1948, geneva, switzerland. lives in geneva.

In **john armleder**'s mixed media works in the 80s, real objects such as electric guitars and couches shared quarters with geometric paintings. His interest in the reverberation between painting and commercial design continues in current two-dimensional work. **GOG**, a suite of 13 silkscreen prints, embodies an unabashed use of graphic design technique—e.g. spot varnishing—and creates optical effects as attention-grabbing as a beacon announcing a club opening. A nevertheless minimal, Warholian seriality informs this portfolio, with colors shifting from print to print, including an extreme Malevichian white-on-white and Reinhardtian black-on-black.

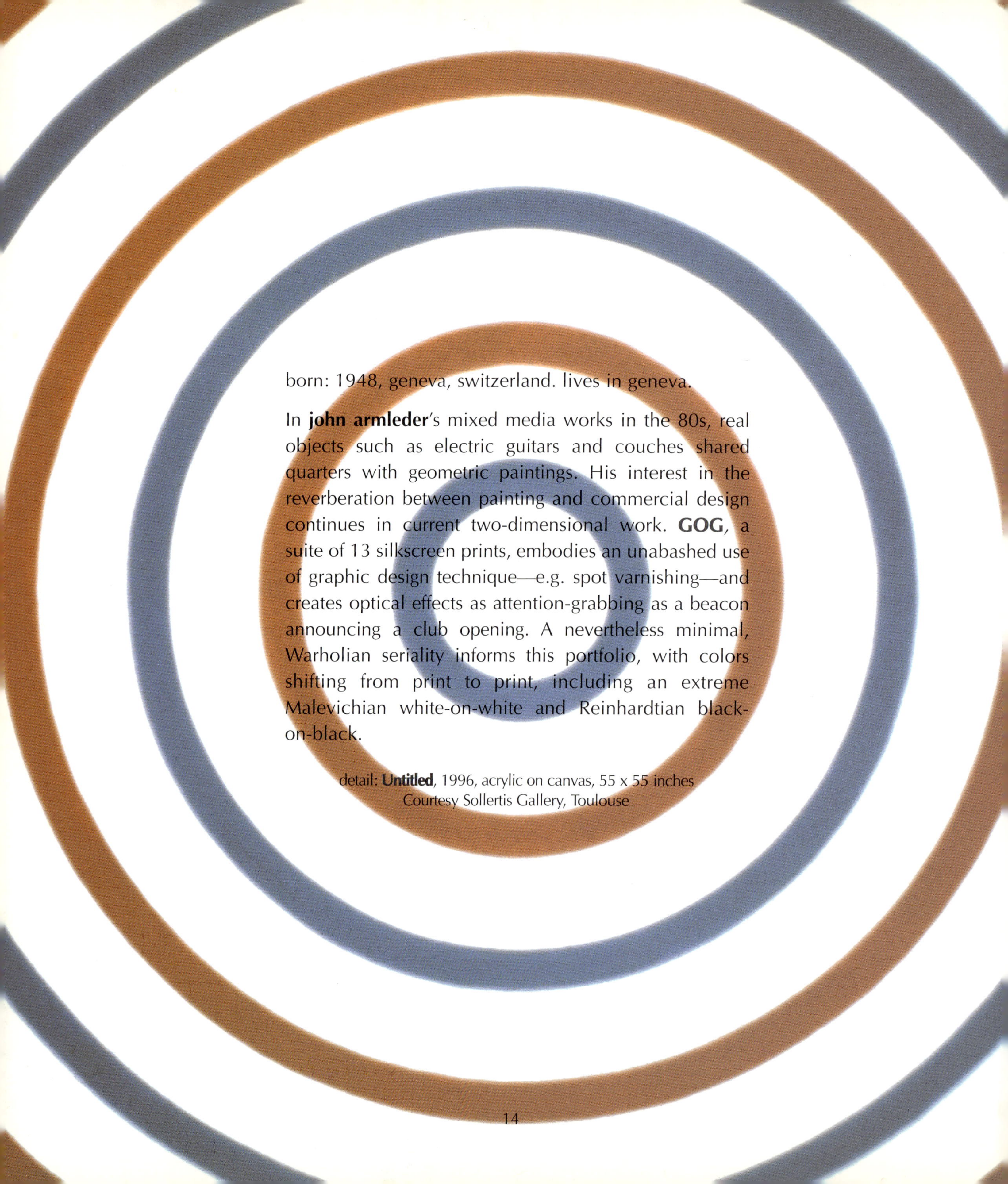

detail: **Untitled**, 1996, acrylic on canvas, 55 x 55 inches
Courtesy Sollertis Gallery, Toulouse

born: 1949, new york. lives in new york.

ross bleckner's ironic appropriation of Op art—a style whose quick rise and fall, according to Peter Halley, mirrored the planned obsolescence of consumer capitalism[1] —had a profound influence on the "Neo-Geo" artists of the mid-1980s, a loosely-defined group that included Halley. Anticipating their "simulationist" aesthetic, which saw capitalist culture as a series of "hyperrealized" retreads of past movements, Bleckner enhanced the fairly straightforward facture of Op—hard edges, flat colors—with a bevy of illusionistic tricks, such as soft-focus edges, creating a sharper edge when viewed from the distance than if the edges were hard to begin with, and painted-in glints of the "illusory" color between the tightly spaced lines.[2] Yet, for all their roots in the simulacrum, the stripes—flickering and wavering like fluorescent tubes, with phantom diamond shapes shooting across the canvas—are sensuous and painterly, with a light that seems to come "from an unknown source, half numinous and half neon."[3]

[1]See Peter Halley, "Ross Bleckner: Painting at the End of History," *Arts*, May 1982, pp. 132-133.
[2]This effect anticipates both Philip Taaffe's "colorized" swirls and David Clarkson's ersatz afterimages.
[3]Gregory Galligan, "Is There Life beyond Neo-Geo? New York Painters," *Art International*, Spring 1989, p. 34.

detail: **The Forest**, 1981, oil on canvas, 120 x 96 inches
Rubell Family Collection, Miami

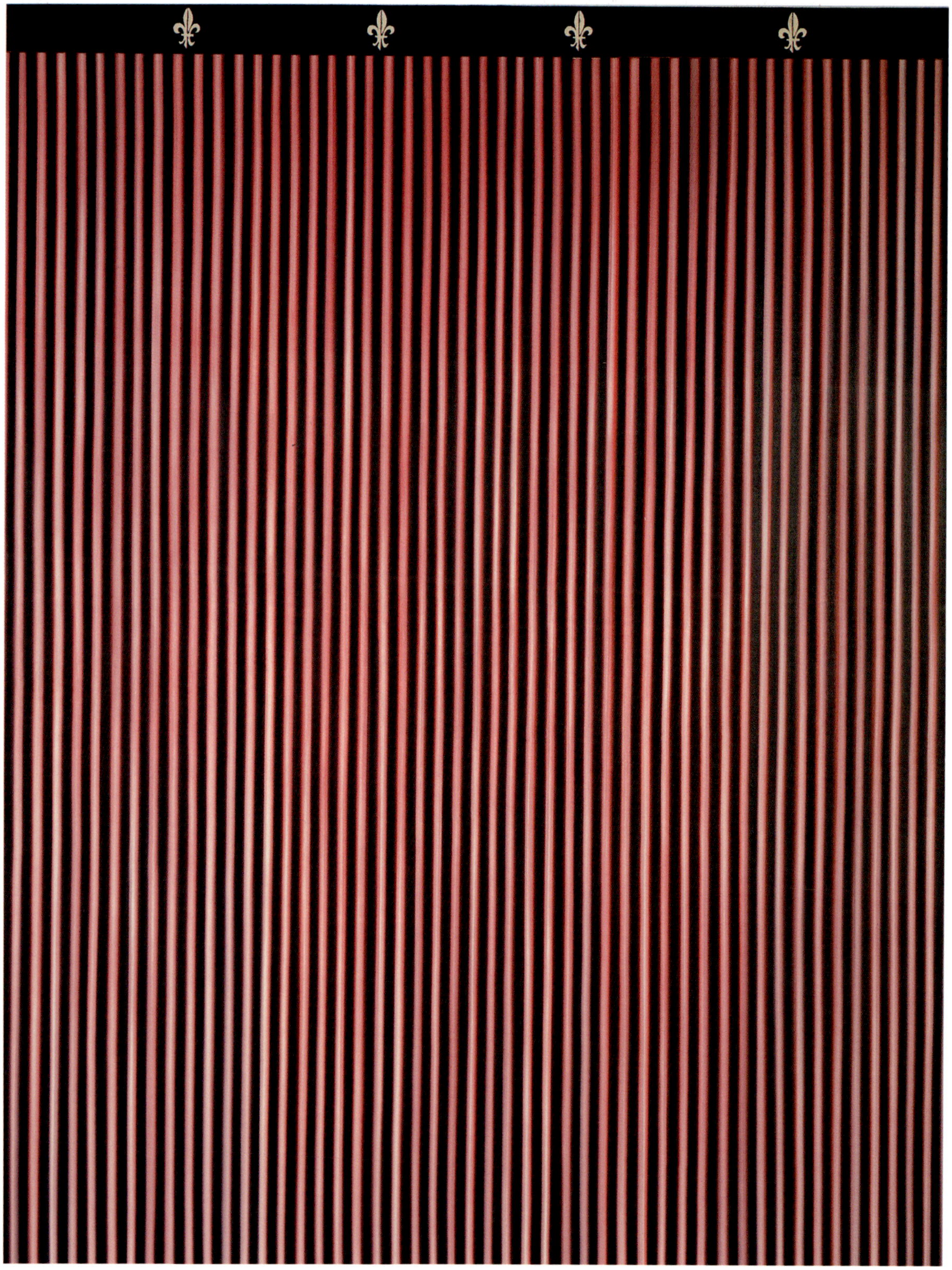

ross bleckner

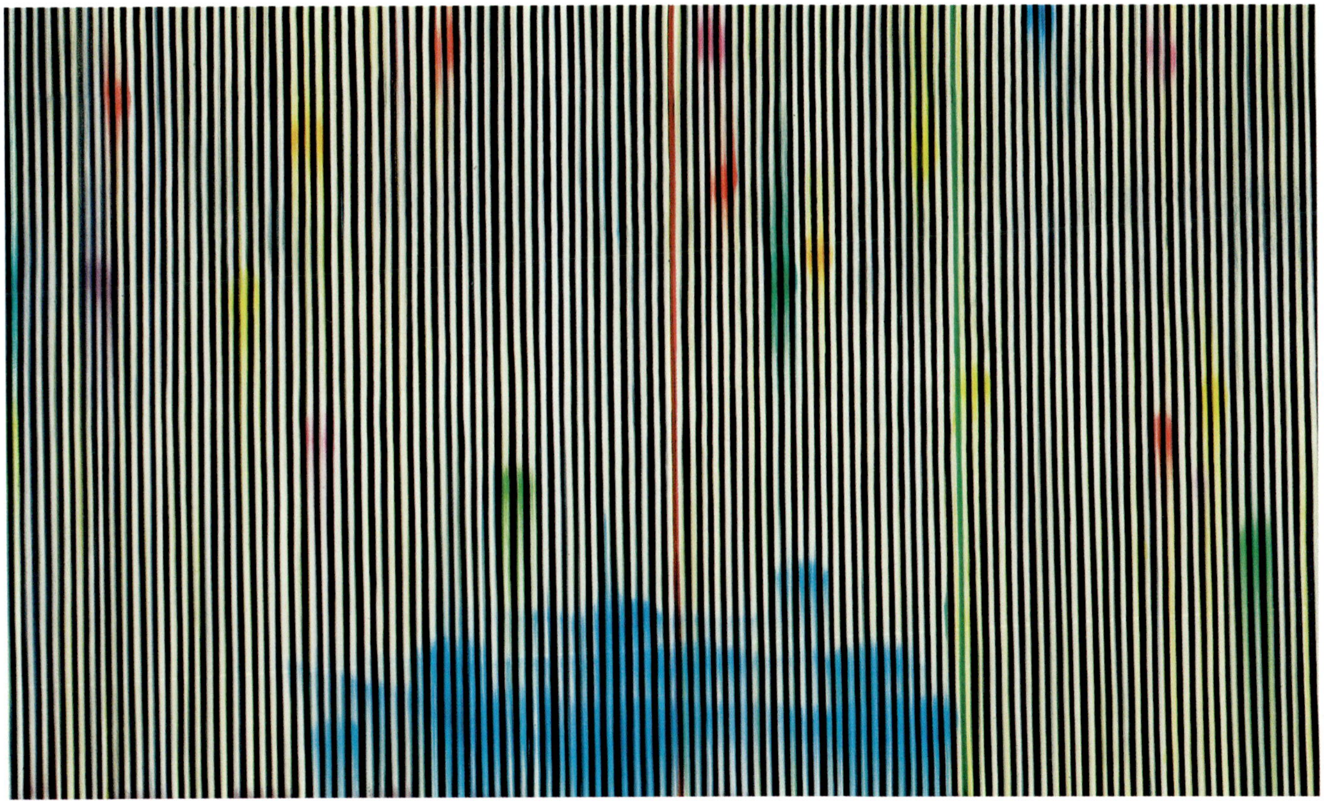

The Arrangement of Things, 1982, oil on canvas, 96 x 162 inches
opposite: **Brothers' Swords**, 1986, oil on canvas, 108 x 84 inches

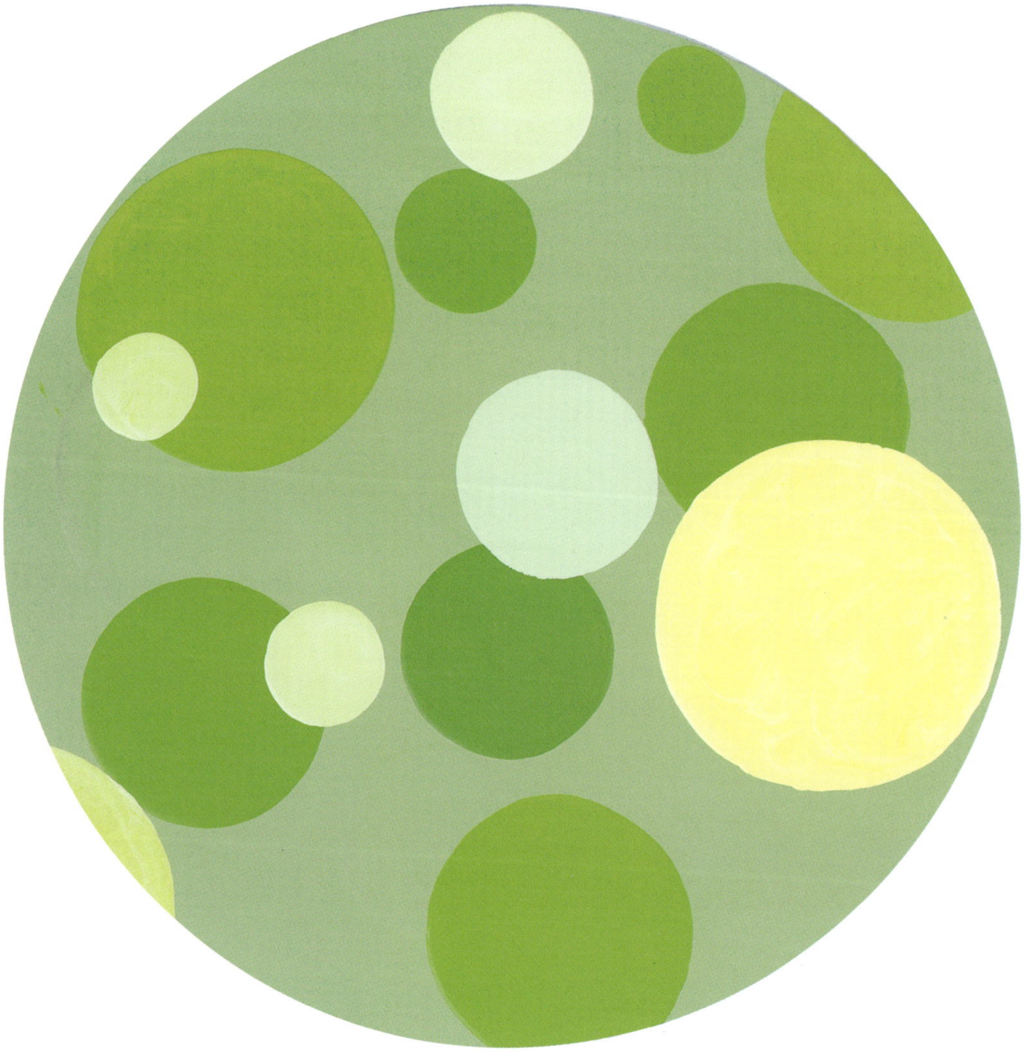

Untitled #29, 1998, acrylic polymer and pigment on wood,12 7/8 inches diameter

stratton cherouny

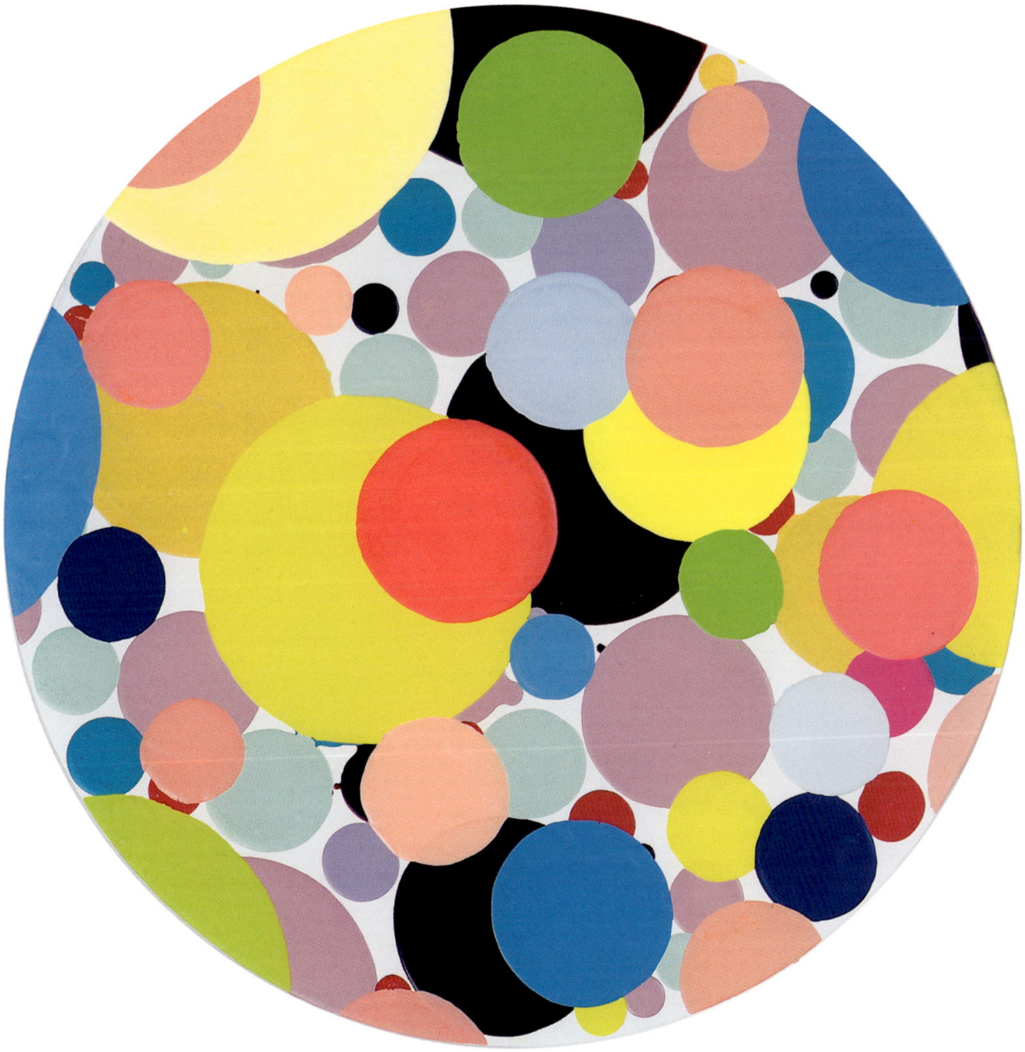

Untitled #34, 1998, acrylic polymer and pigment on wood,12 7/8 inches diameter

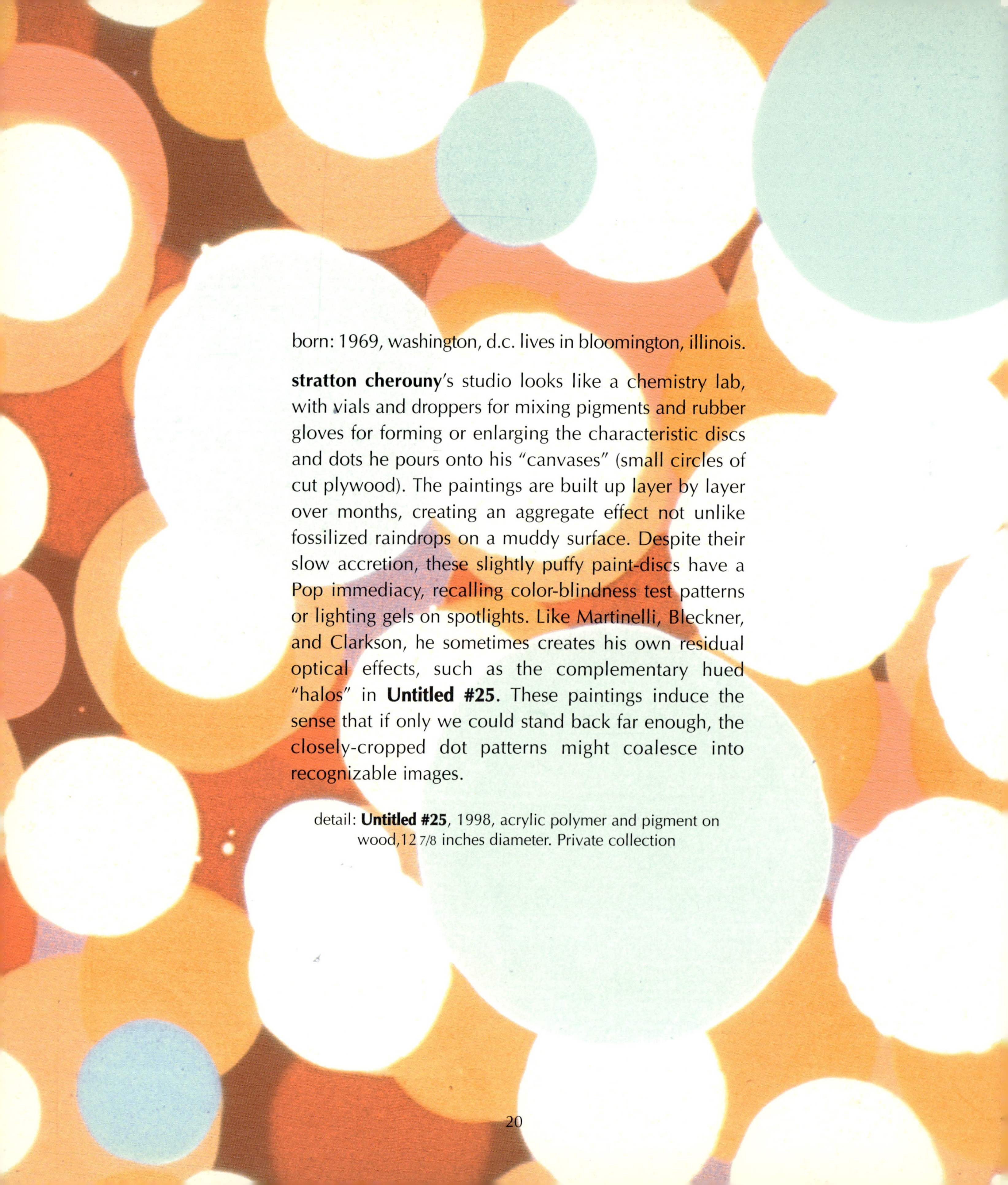

born: 1969, washington, d.c. lives in bloomington, illinois.

stratton cherouny's studio looks like a chemistry lab, with vials and droppers for mixing pigments and rubber gloves for forming or enlarging the characteristic discs and dots he pours onto his "canvases" (small circles of cut plywood). The paintings are built up layer by layer over months, creating an aggregate effect not unlike fossilized raindrops on a muddy surface. Despite their slow accretion, these slightly puffy paint-discs have a Pop immediacy, recalling color-blindness test patterns or lighting gels on spotlights. Like Martinelli, Bleckner, and Clarkson, he sometimes creates his own residual optical effects, such as the complementary hued "halos" in **Untitled #25.** These paintings induce the sense that if only we could stand back far enough, the closely-cropped dot patterns might coalesce into recognizable images.

detail: **Untitled #25**, 1998, acrylic polymer and pigment on wood, 12 7/8 inches diameter. Private collection

born: 1958, ottawa. lives in new york.

david clarkson explores the semiotics of painting in a playful, seductive way, turning aspects of the viewing experience normally overlooked by the audience into a series of caricature-like symbols. A highlight on a monochrome panel, for example, appears as a cartoon oval in the upper left corner, while a cast shadow is represented by a dark, slightly wavy strip of wood attached to the painting's bottom edge. The glowing red light bulbs affixed to his "afterimage" paintings are meant to invoke light sources that create afterimages—the ghostly *doppelgangers* appearing on the retina in response to bright light—while the clusters of dots spray painted on the panels represent the afterimages themselves. The irony is that the color contrast between the dots and their background makes the fake afterimages much more optically charged (i.e. afterimage-producing) than the low-wattage bulbs. In recent pieces such as **Iris Seventh Avenue Style**, Clarkson further complicates the work by integrating the bulbs and ersatz afterimages into Jasper Johnsian targets and skewed Vasarelian grids.

detail: **Retina Painting**, 1998, enamel, light bulbs on wood, 24 x 20 x 3 inches
Courtesy the artist

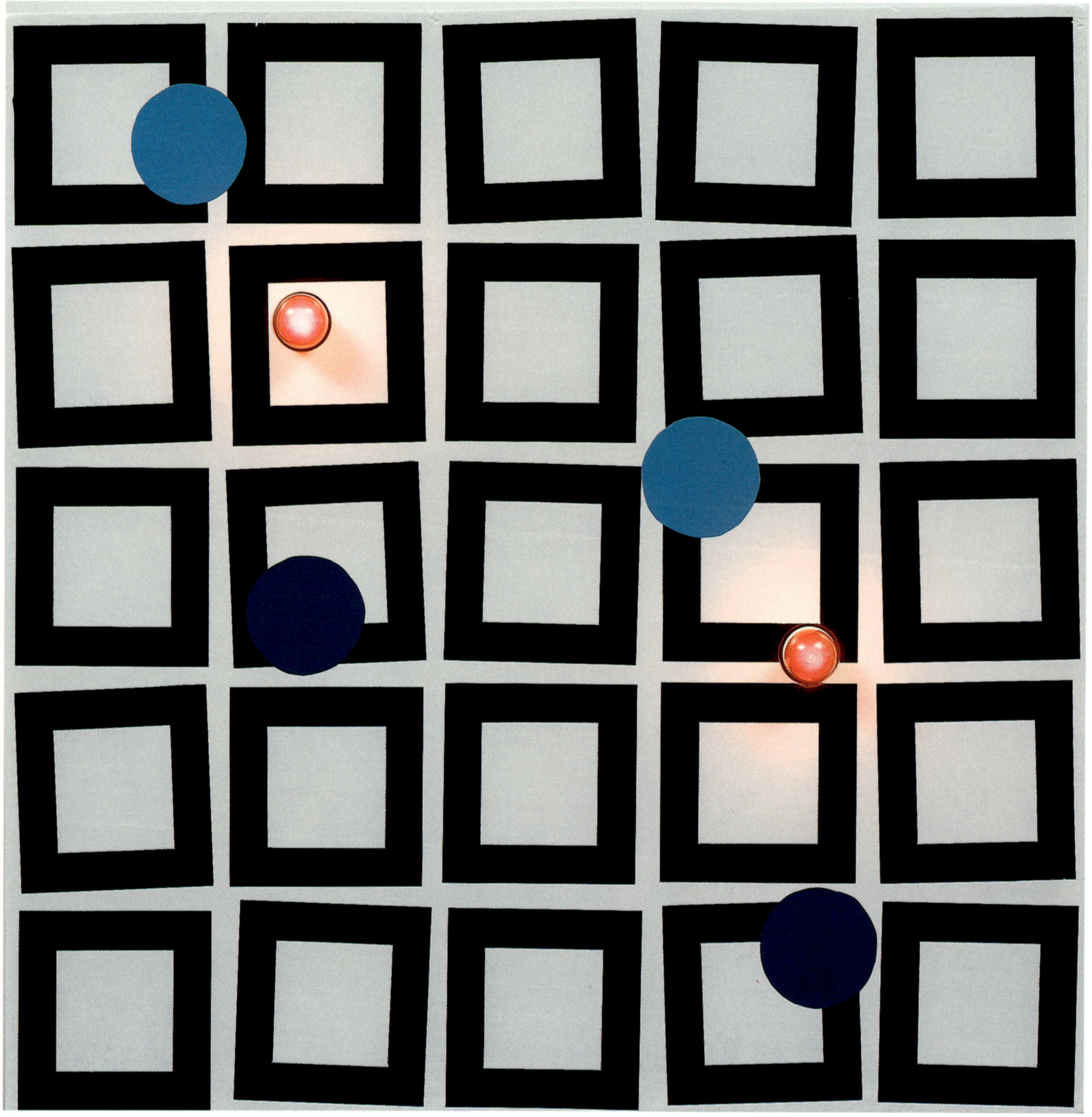

Performance-enhanced, 1998, enamel on wood with lightbulbs, 28 x 28 x 2 inches

david clarkson

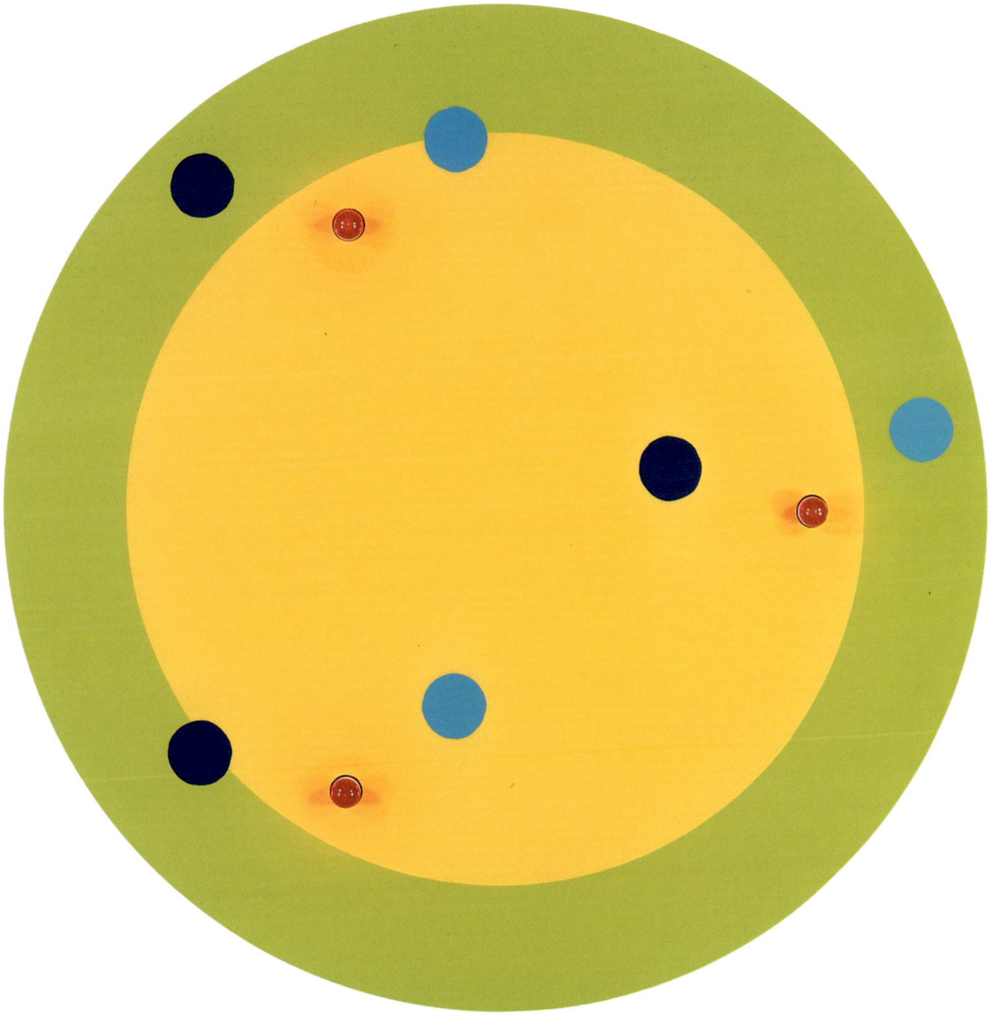

Iris Seventh Avenue Style, 1998, enamel on wood with light bulbs, 47 inches diameter x 2 inches

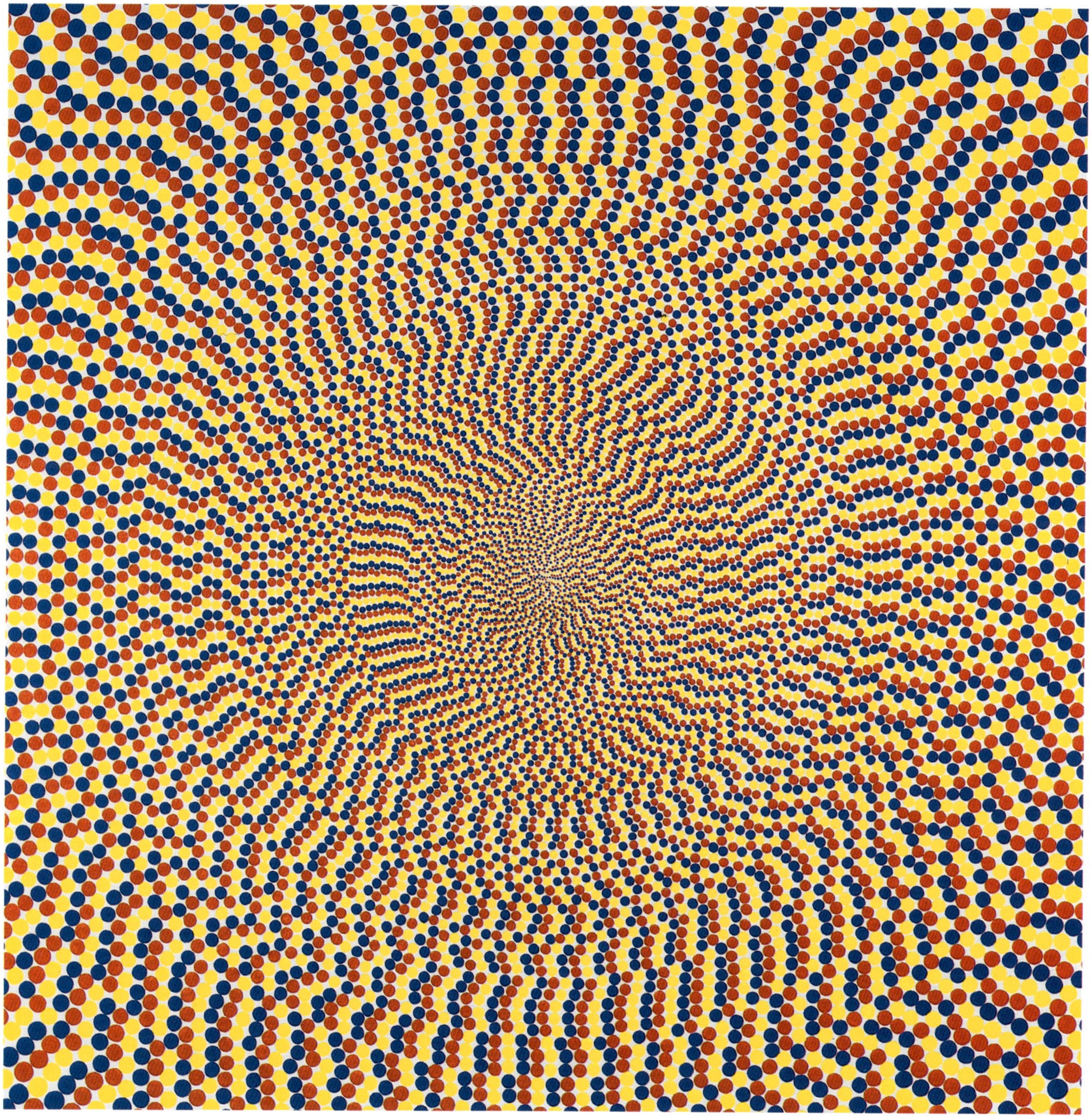

mark dagley

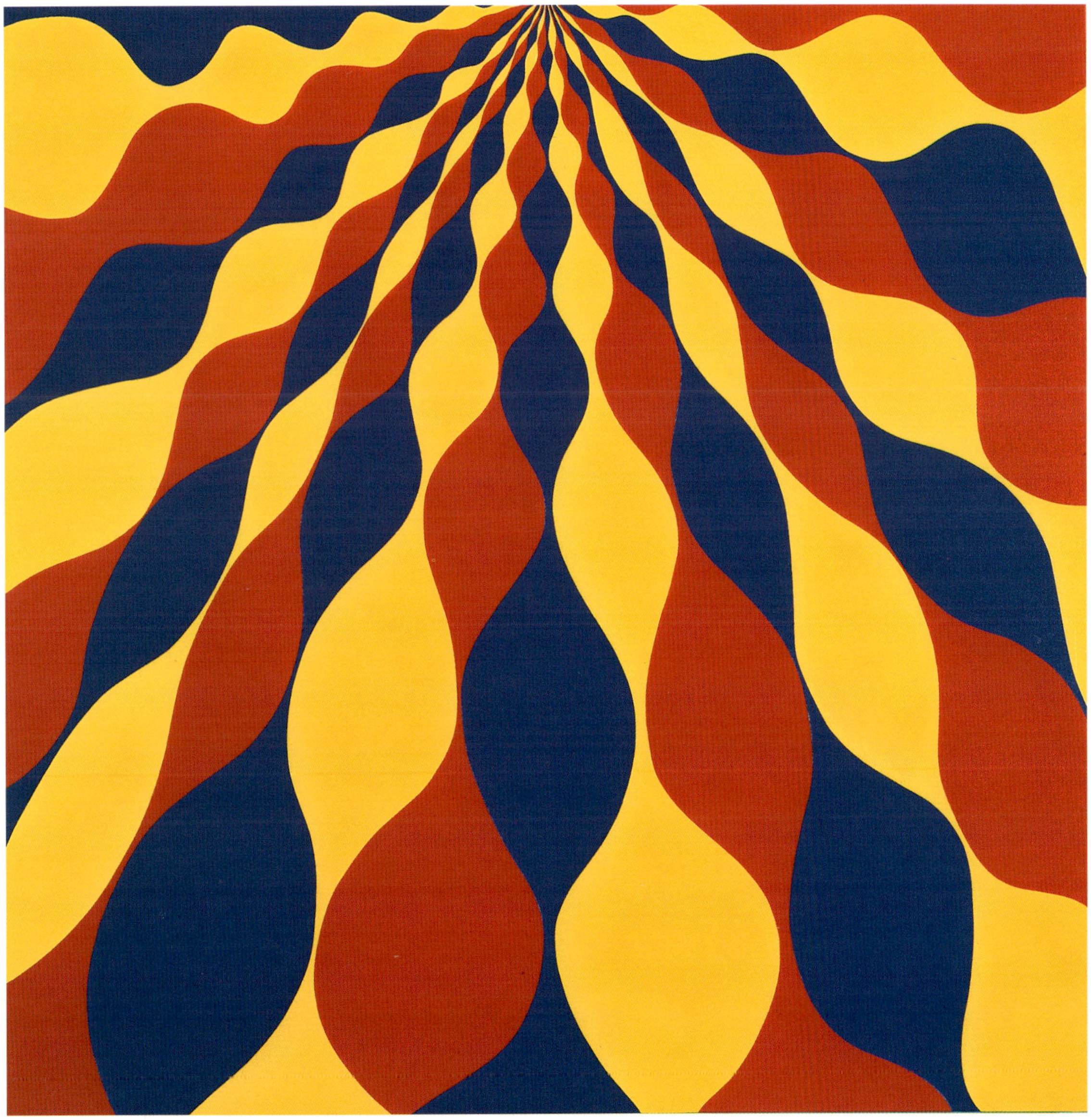

Primary Color Vortex, 1995, acrylic on canvas, 72 x 72 inches
opposite: **Concentric Sequence**, 1996, acrylic and pencil on canvas, 72 x 72 inches

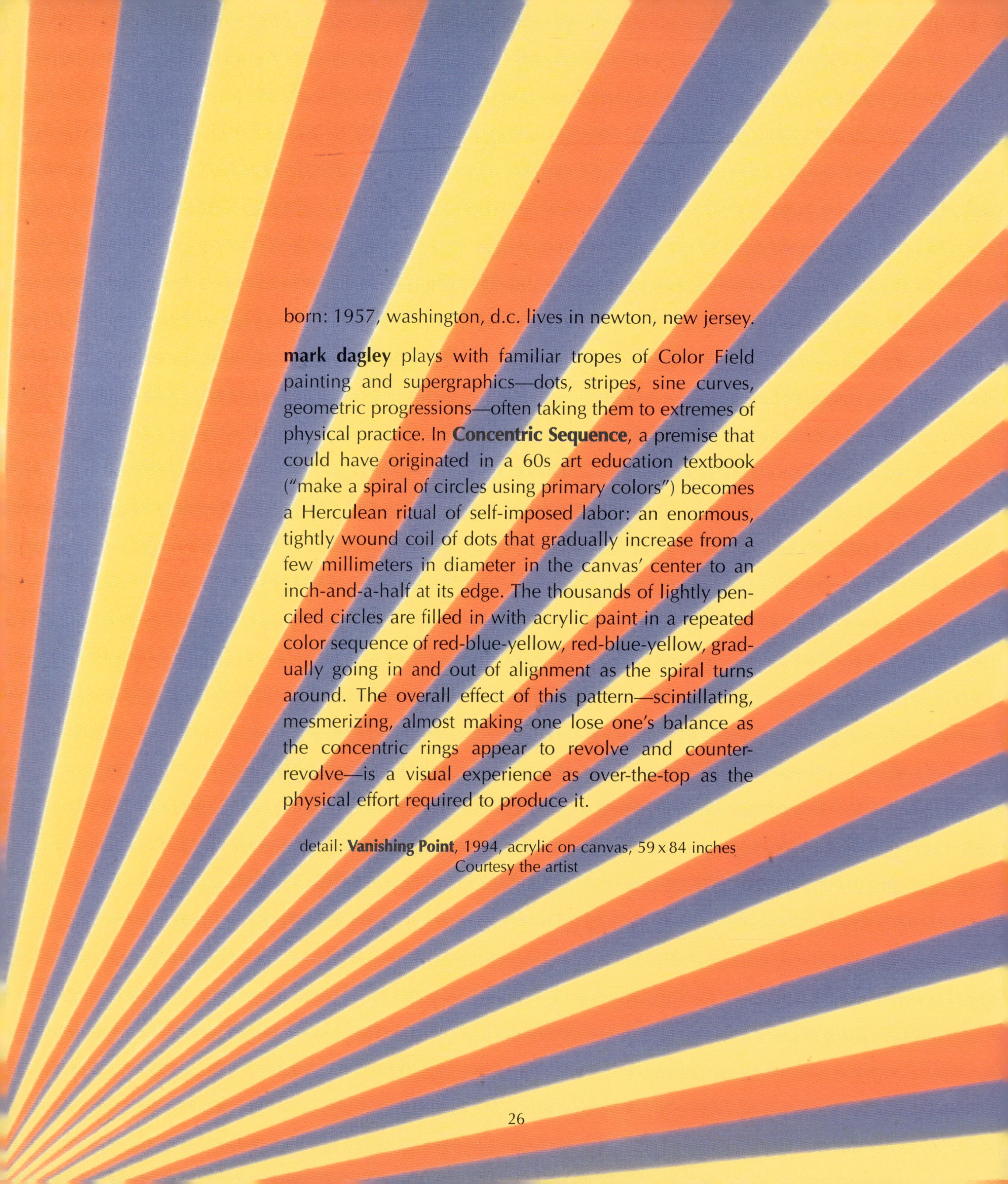

born: 1957, washington, d.c. lives in newton, new jersey.

mark dagley plays with familiar tropes of Color Field painting and supergraphics—dots, stripes, sine curves, geometric progressions—often taking them to extremes of physical practice. In **Concentric Sequence**, a premise that could have originated in a 60s art education textbook ("make a spiral of circles using primary colors") becomes a Herculean ritual of self-imposed labor: an enormous, tightly wound coil of dots that gradually increase from a few millimeters in diameter in the canvas' center to an inch-and-a-half at its edge. The thousands of lightly penciled circles are filled in with acrylic paint in a repeated color sequence of red-blue-yellow, red-blue-yellow, gradually going in and out of alignment as the spiral turns around. The overall effect of this pattern—scintillating, mesmerizing, almost making one lose one's balance as the concentric rings appear to revolve and counter-revolve—is a visual experience as over-the-top as the physical effort required to produce it.

detail: **Vanishing Point**, 1994, acrylic on canvas, 59 x 84 inches
Courtesy the artist

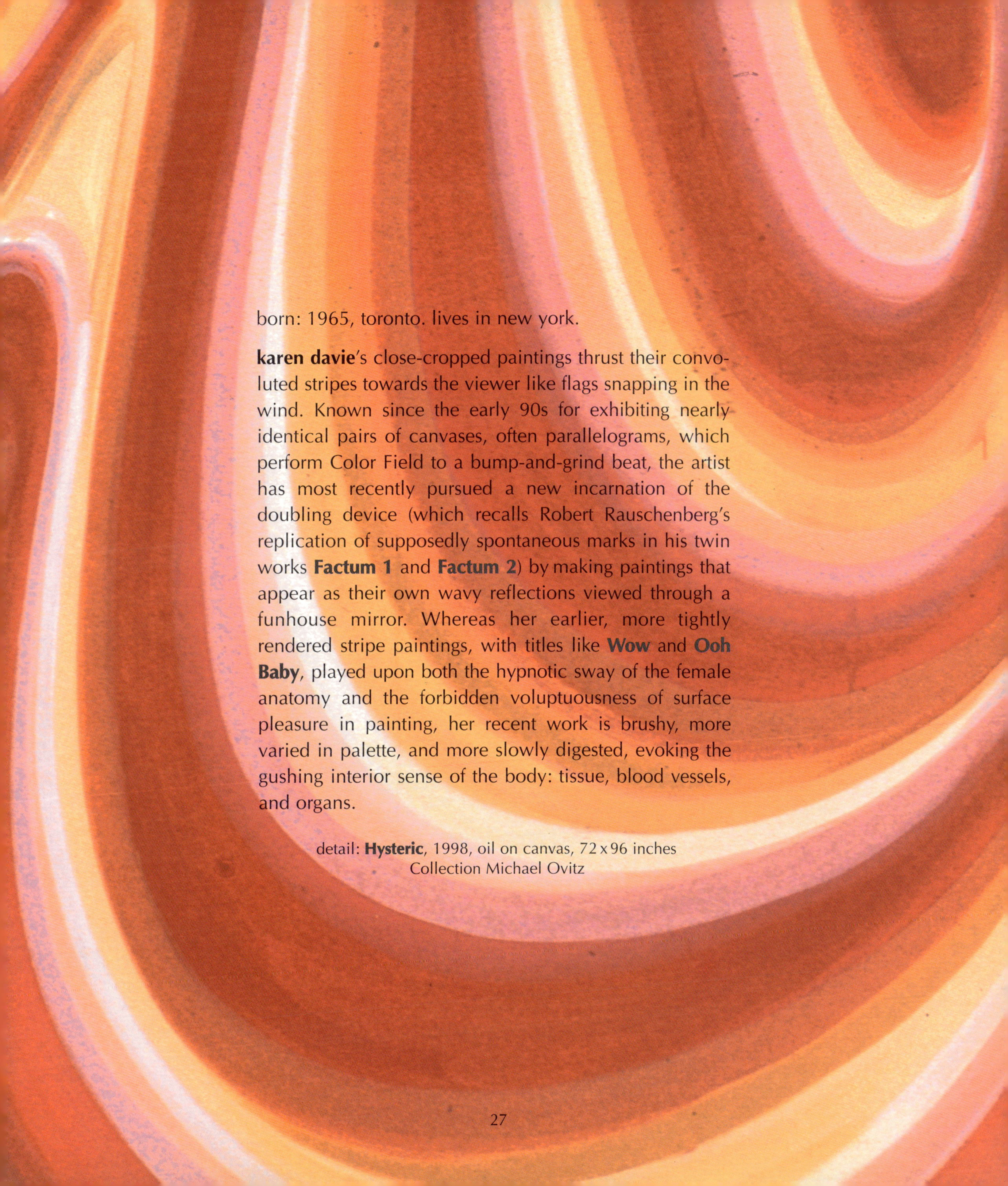

born: 1965, toronto. lives in new york.

karen davie's close-cropped paintings thrust their convoluted stripes towards the viewer like flags snapping in the wind. Known since the early 90s for exhibiting nearly identical pairs of canvases, often parallelograms, which perform Color Field to a bump-and-grind beat, the artist has most recently pursued a new incarnation of the doubling device (which recalls Robert Rauschenberg's replication of supposedly spontaneous marks in his twin works **Factum 1** and **Factum 2**) by making paintings that appear as their own wavy reflections viewed through a funhouse mirror. Whereas her earlier, more tightly rendered stripe paintings, with titles like **Wow** and **Ooh Baby**, played upon both the hypnotic sway of the female anatomy and the forbidden voluptuousness of surface pleasure in painting, her recent work is brushy, more varied in palette, and more slowly digested, evoking the gushing interior sense of the body: tissue, blood vessels, and organs.

detail: **Hysteric**, 1998, oil on canvas, 72 x 96 inches
Collection Michael Ovitz

karen davie

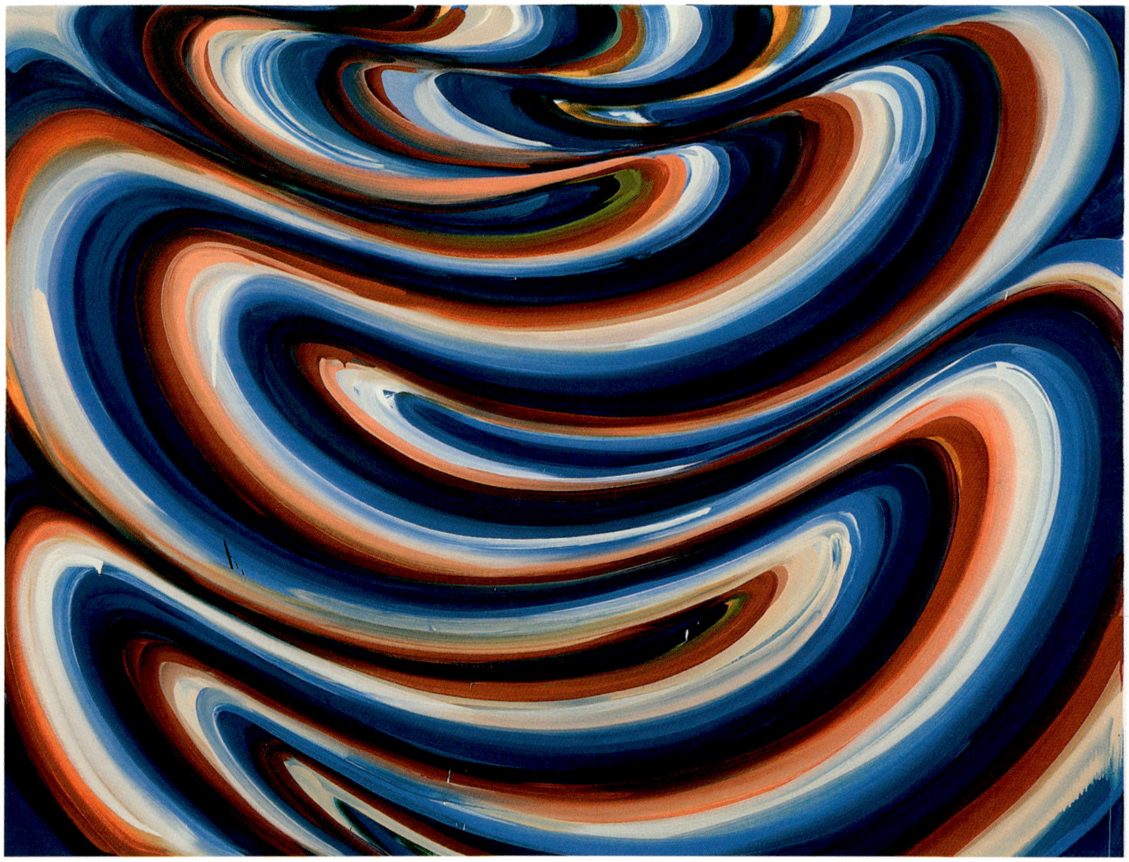

Wanted, 1998, oil on canvas, 72 x 96 inches
opposite: **Over**, 1998, oil on canvas, 72 x 60 inches

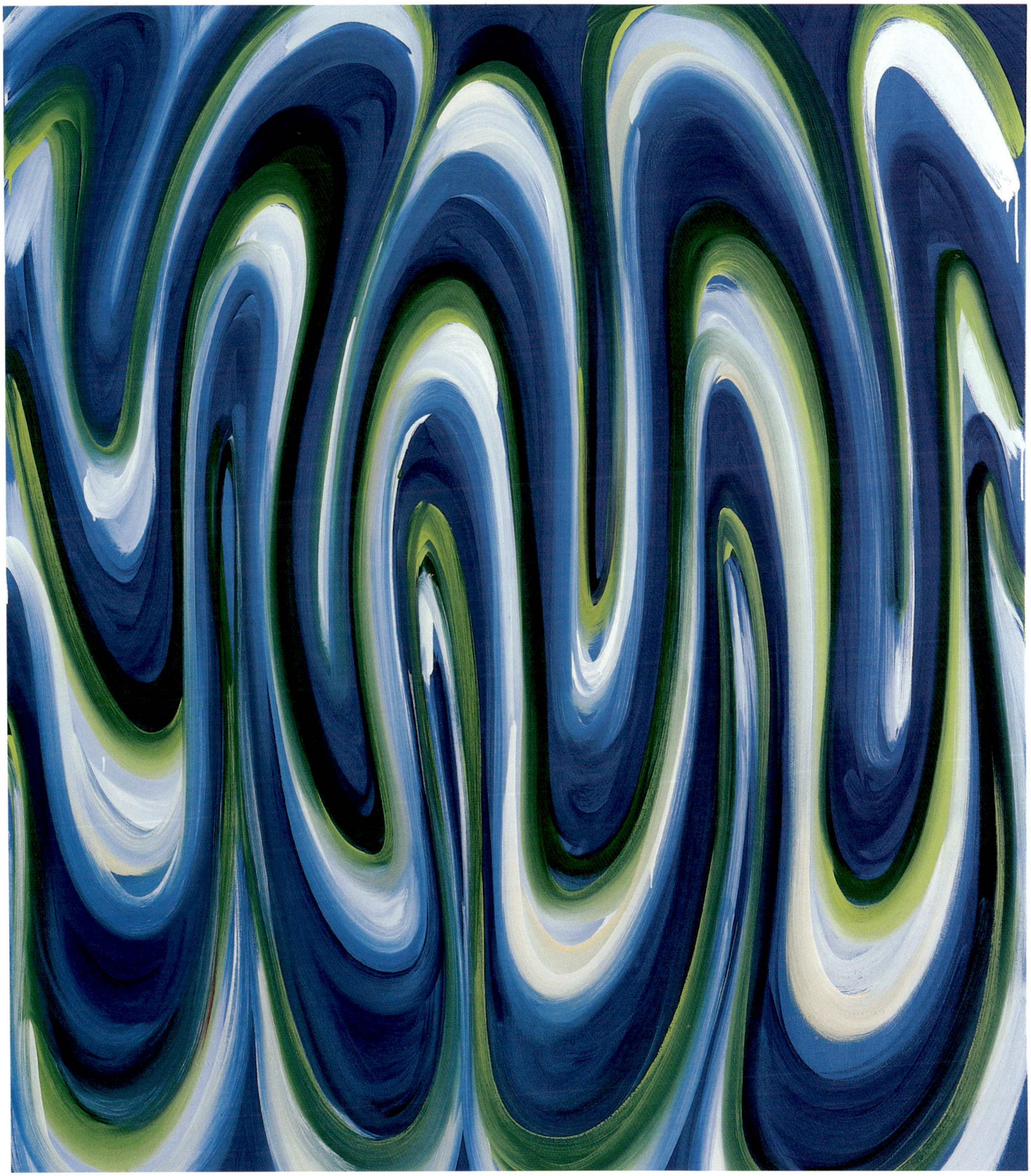

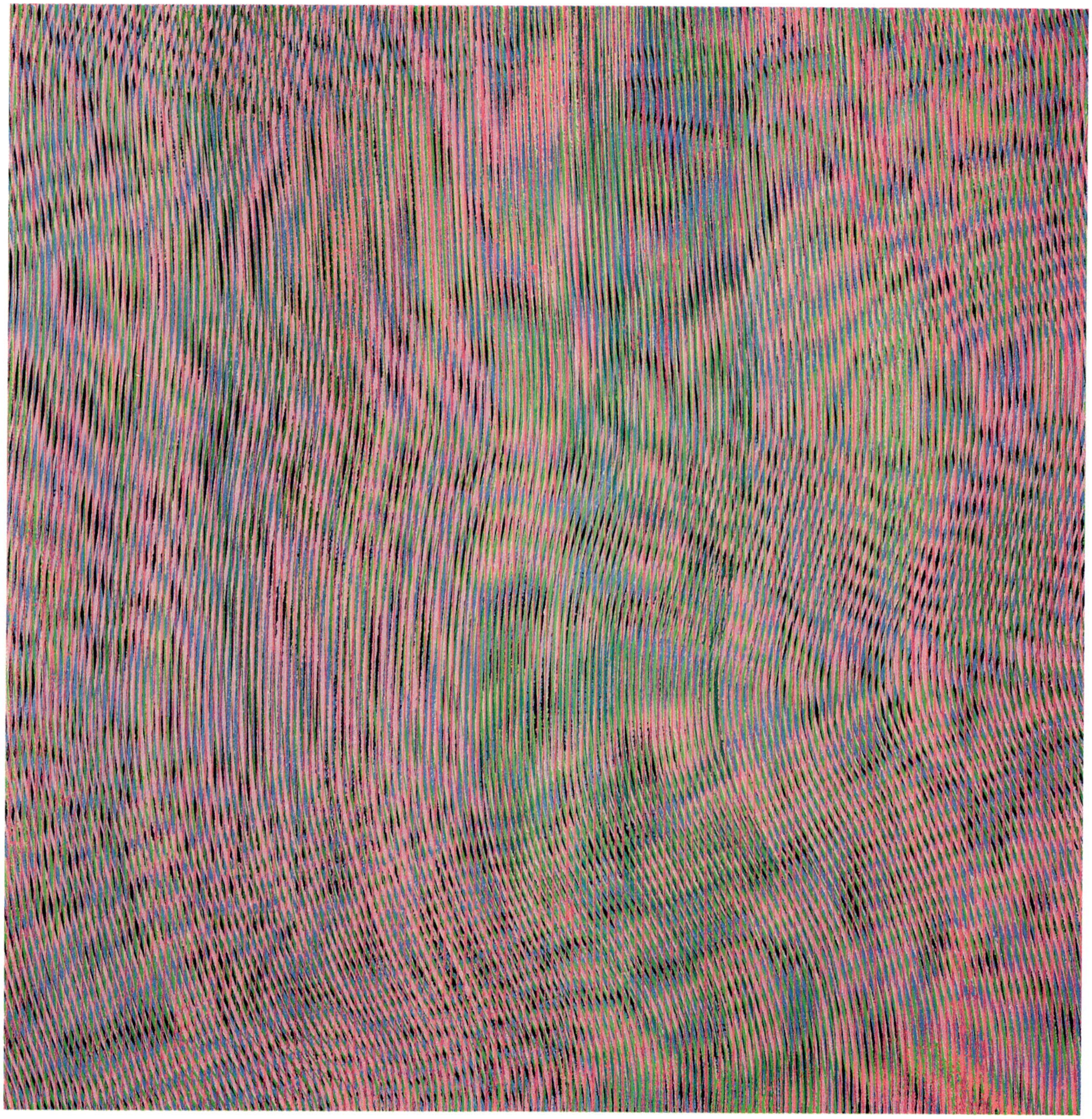

Untitled, 1989, acrylic on canvas, 30 x 30 inches
opposite: **Scan**, 1989, acrylic on canvas, 120 x 42 inches

steve di benedetto

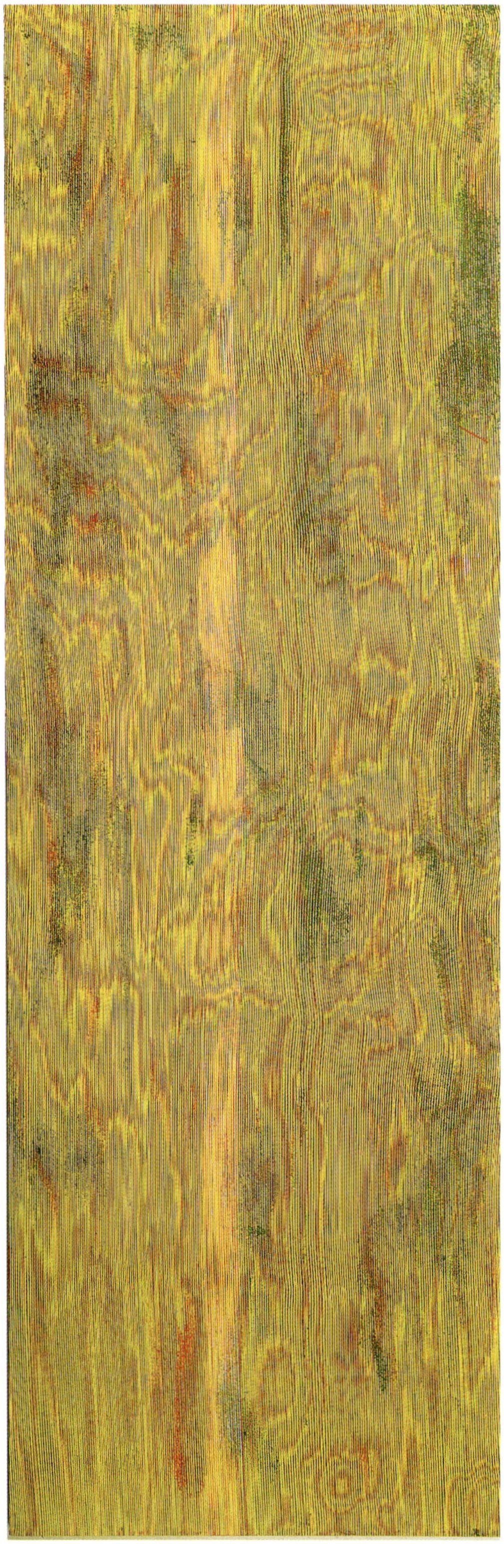

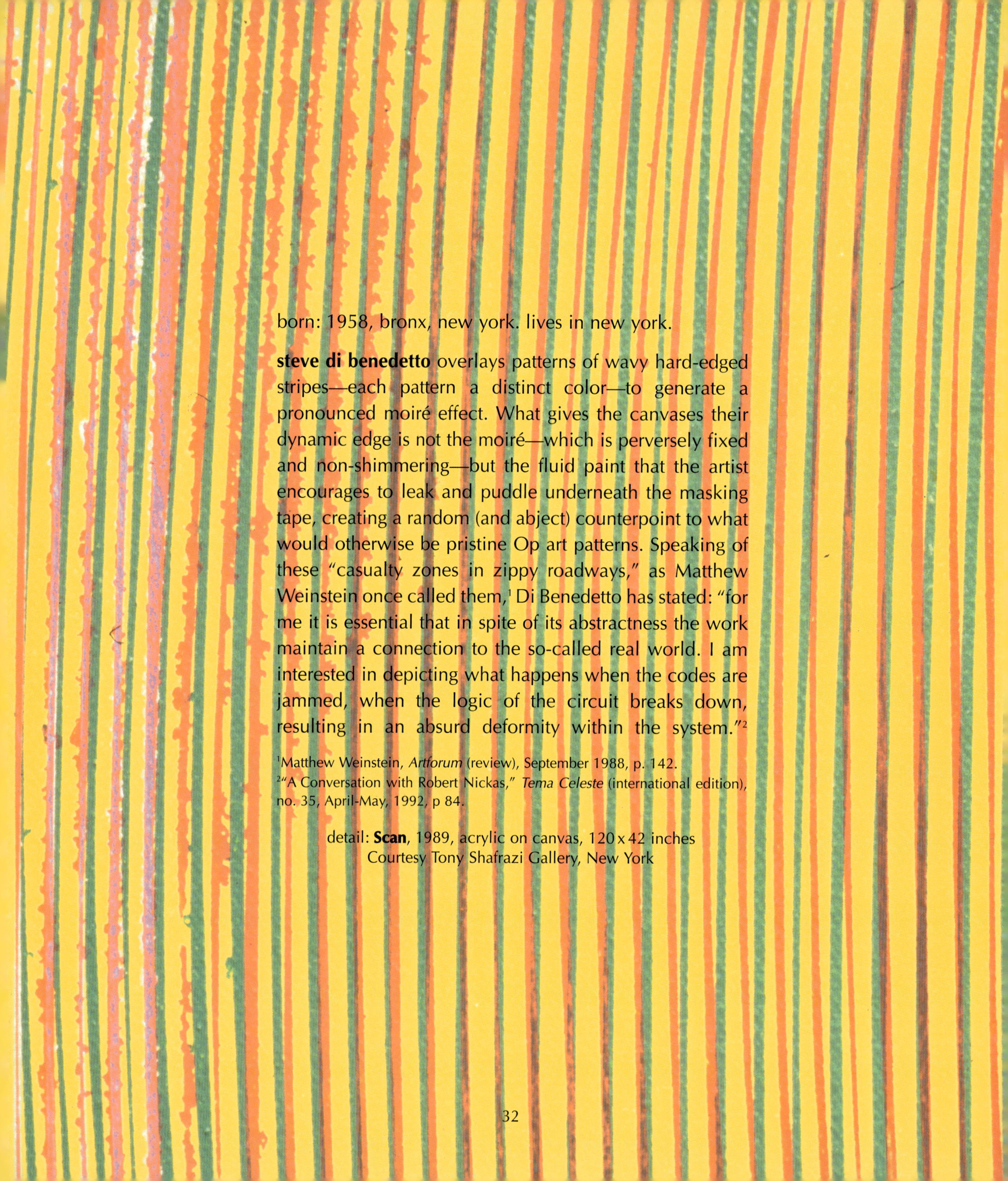

born: 1958, bronx, new york. lives in new york.

steve di benedetto overlays patterns of wavy hard-edged stripes—each pattern a distinct color—to generate a pronounced moiré effect. What gives the canvases their dynamic edge is not the moiré—which is perversely fixed and non-shimmering—but the fluid paint that the artist encourages to leak and puddle underneath the masking tape, creating a random (and abject) counterpoint to what would otherwise be pristine Op art patterns. Speaking of these "casualty zones in zippy roadways," as Matthew Weinstein once called them,[1] Di Benedetto has stated: "for me it is essential that in spite of its abstractness the work maintain a connection to the so-called real world. I am interested in depicting what happens when the codes are jammed, when the logic of the circuit breaks down, resulting in an absurd deformity within the system."[2]

[1]Matthew Weinstein, *Artforum* (review), September 1988, p. 142.
[2]"A Conversation with Robert Nickas," *Tema Celeste* (international edition), no. 35, April-May, 1992, p 84.

detail: **Scan**, 1989, acrylic on canvas, 120 x 42 inches
Courtesy Tony Shafrazi Gallery, New York

born: 1962, oshkosh, wisconsin. lives in chicago.

michelle grabner's paintings appear at first to be Minimalist monochromatic grids (often with shimmering patterns that might be called "soft Op"), but are in fact based on everyday household items such as furnace filters, blankets, place mats, curtains, grapefruit bags, and the stitched backs of rugs. Using these found materials as stencils, Grabner spray-paints the patterns onto thin plywood panels and then fills in the "negative" spaces by hand with enamel paint. In contrast to Op's and Minimalism's studio-based hermeticism, Grabner's works—painted on a kitchen tabletop—are like seismographs monitoring the physical and psychological quirks of the home environment. On the physical side, her patterns wobble as the lines in them meander and are interrupted by stains and other defects in the stencilled materials.[1] On the psychological side, one learns that her designs "become more meticulous and perfect when she is under physical and emotional stress, and more adventurous when other aspects of her daily life are under control."[2]

[1]James Yood, *Artforum* (review), Summer 1996, p. 112.
[2]Eugene Tan, *Contemporary Visual Arts*, Issue 19 (Summer 1998), p. 67.

detail: **Daisy Tile**, 1996, enamel on panel, 32 x 38 inches
Courtesy Richard Heller Gallery, Santa Monica

michelle grabner

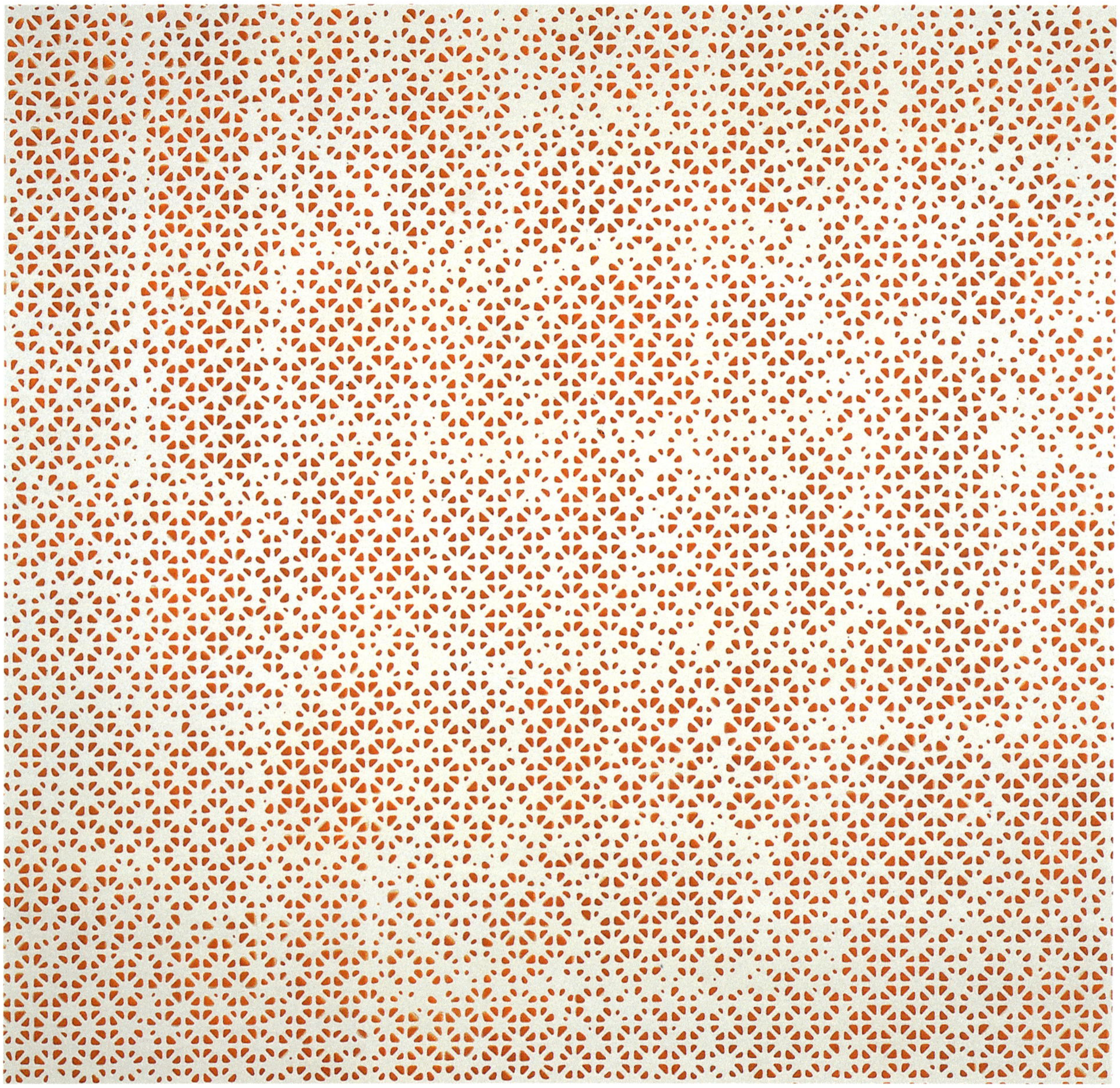

Screen #2 (orange), 1998-99, enamel on medex, 32 x 34 inches
opposite: **Fuzzy Blkt #4**, 1998, enamel and flock/medex, 28 x 24 inches

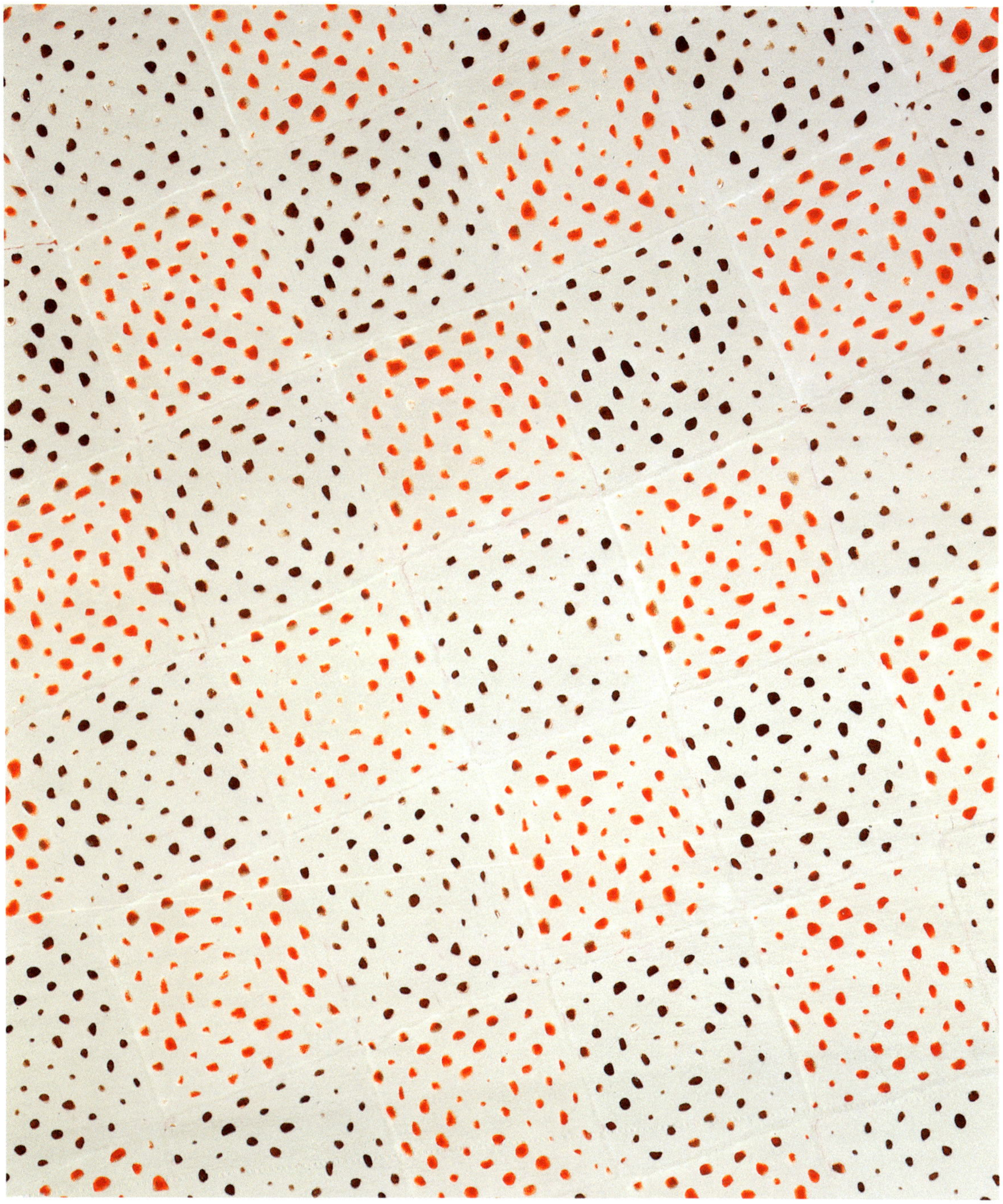

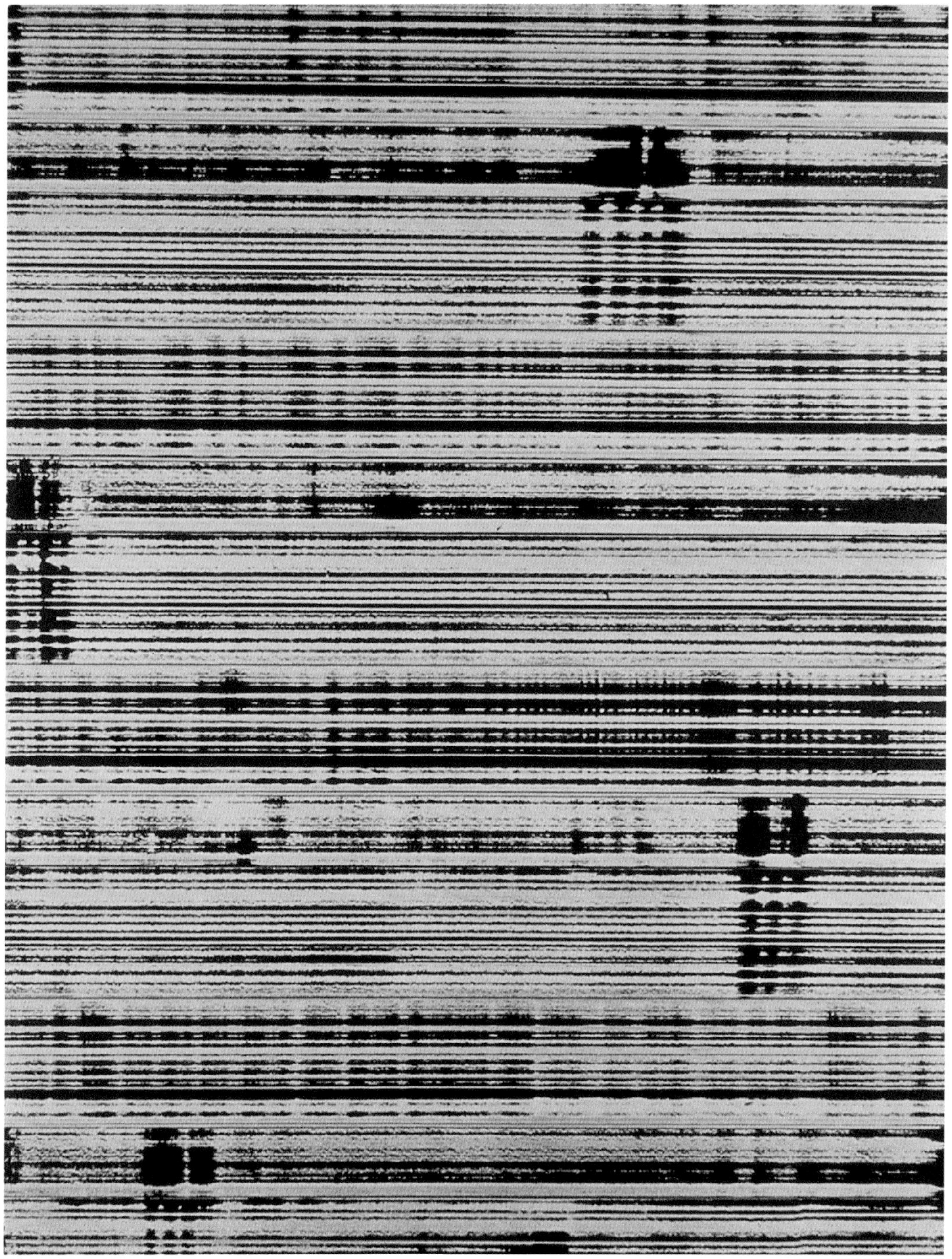

tad griffin

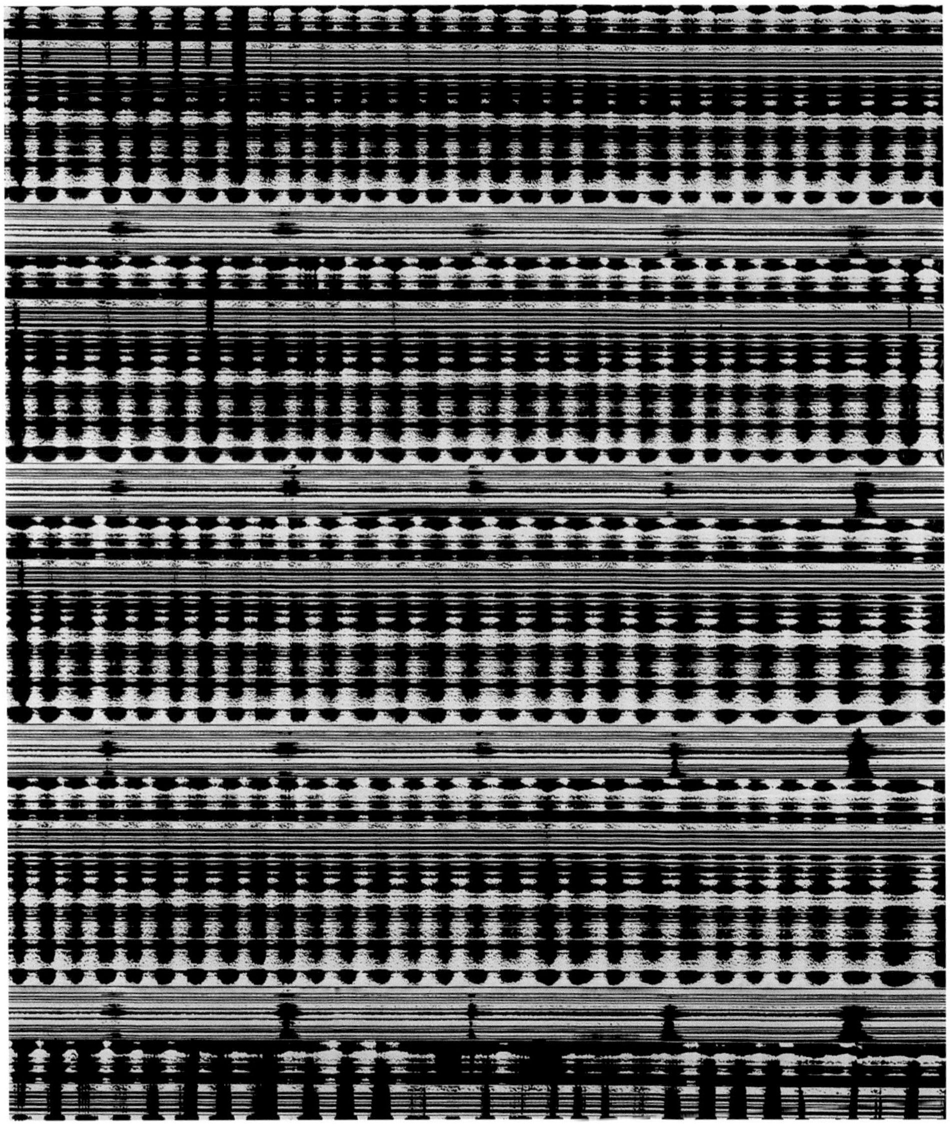

Echolate 8, 1994, oil on canvas, 82 x 72 inches
opposite: **Untitled L**, 1995, oil on canvas, 72 x 56 inches

born: 1966, houston. lives in houston.

tad griffin's rhythmic arrays of tightly spaced horizontal lines with taut, photo-emulsion-like surfaces bridge the gap between Op art, gestural abstraction, and technical ephemera such as seismographs and EEGs. To achieve this high-speed digital look, the artist drags paint with specially fabricated squeegees across a gessoed, sanded canvas, leaving hundreds of thick and thin lines punctuated with quasi-xerographic "static." In Griffin's dystopian universe, these cool robotic marks—also recalling Warhol's photo-silkscreens (particularly the Atomic Bombs and other serial paintings)—are all that remains of the abstract gestures of yesteryear: as the artist notes, "the romantic associations of the mark as personal record are effectively negated."

detail: **Echolate 1**, 1994, oil on canvas, 82 x 72 inches
Courtesy the artist and Texas Gallery, Houston

born: 1953, new york city. lives in new york.

The cells and conduits that recur in **peter halley**'s paintings are all-purpose metaphors: they can be read as computer chips, flow charts, road systems, or rooms with utility and communication lines going in and out. His Day-Glo and acrylic colors mimic the attention-grabbing hues of advertising and packaging, and the cells typically have the granular texture of fake stucco, which Halley says is reminiscent of "motel ceilings." These stylistic elements address Jean Baudrillard's idea of the "simulacrum" as a guiding principle in late 20th century culture, but the paintings' combination of intrusive scale, startling color choices, social satire, comic book immediacy, and outrageous juxtapositions of texture gives them a vitality and edginess that goes beyond the mere illustration of theory. The paintings are "double coded," to use a term of architect and postmodern theorist Charles Jencks, questioning the assumptions of the society in which they are produced while appealing to viewers on a material, experiential level.

Excerpted from Tom Moody, "Peter Halley and the Reagan Era," exhibition brochure for "Encounters 6," Dallas Museum of Art, 1995.

detail: **Shonen Knife**, 1991, acrylic, Day-Glo acrylic and Roll-a-Tex on canvas, 86 1/4 x 85 1/2. The Sternberg Collection, Chicago

peter halley

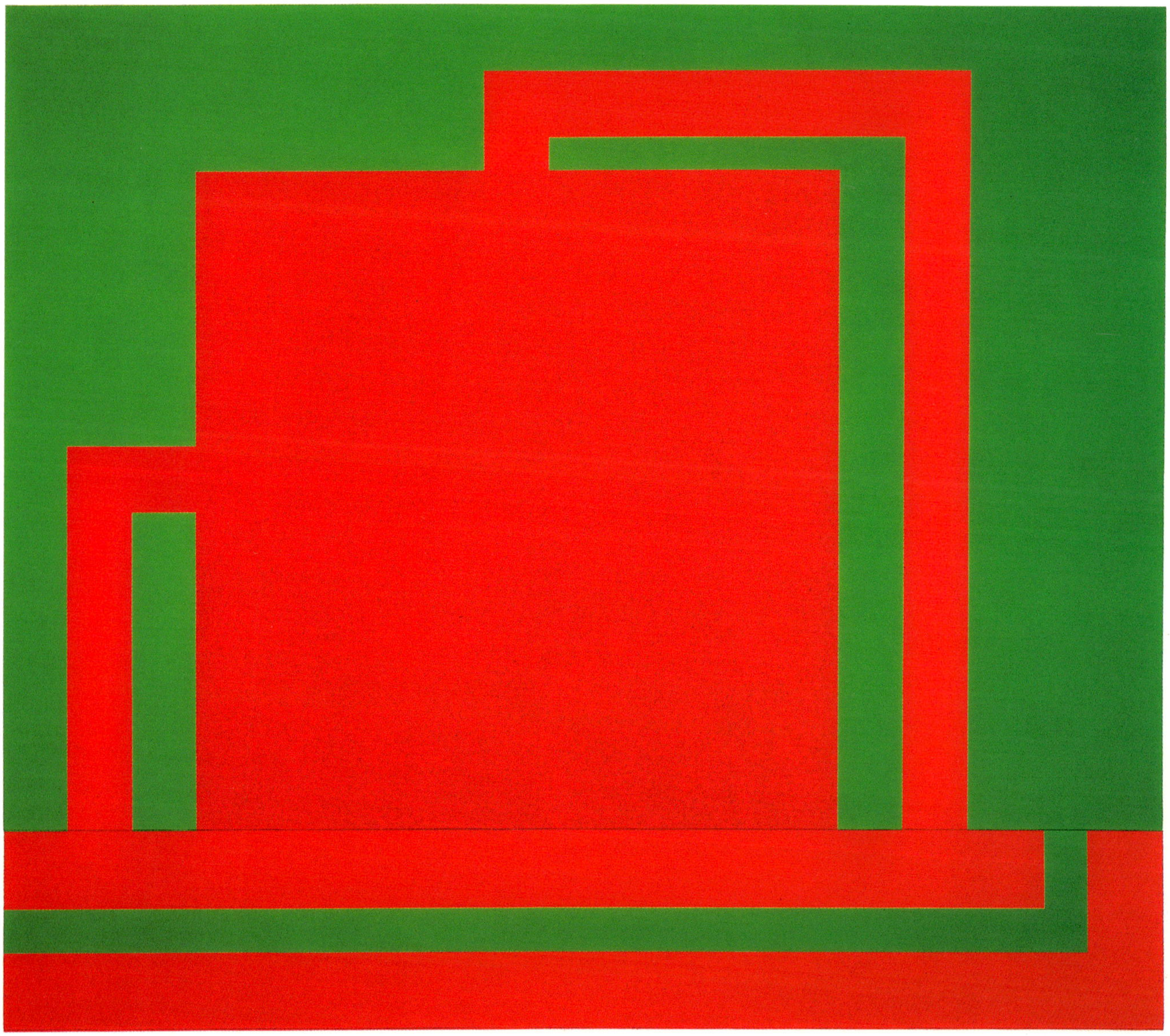

Red Cell, 1988, acrylic, Day-Glo acrylic, Roll-a-Tex on canvas, 93 x 108 x 3 inches

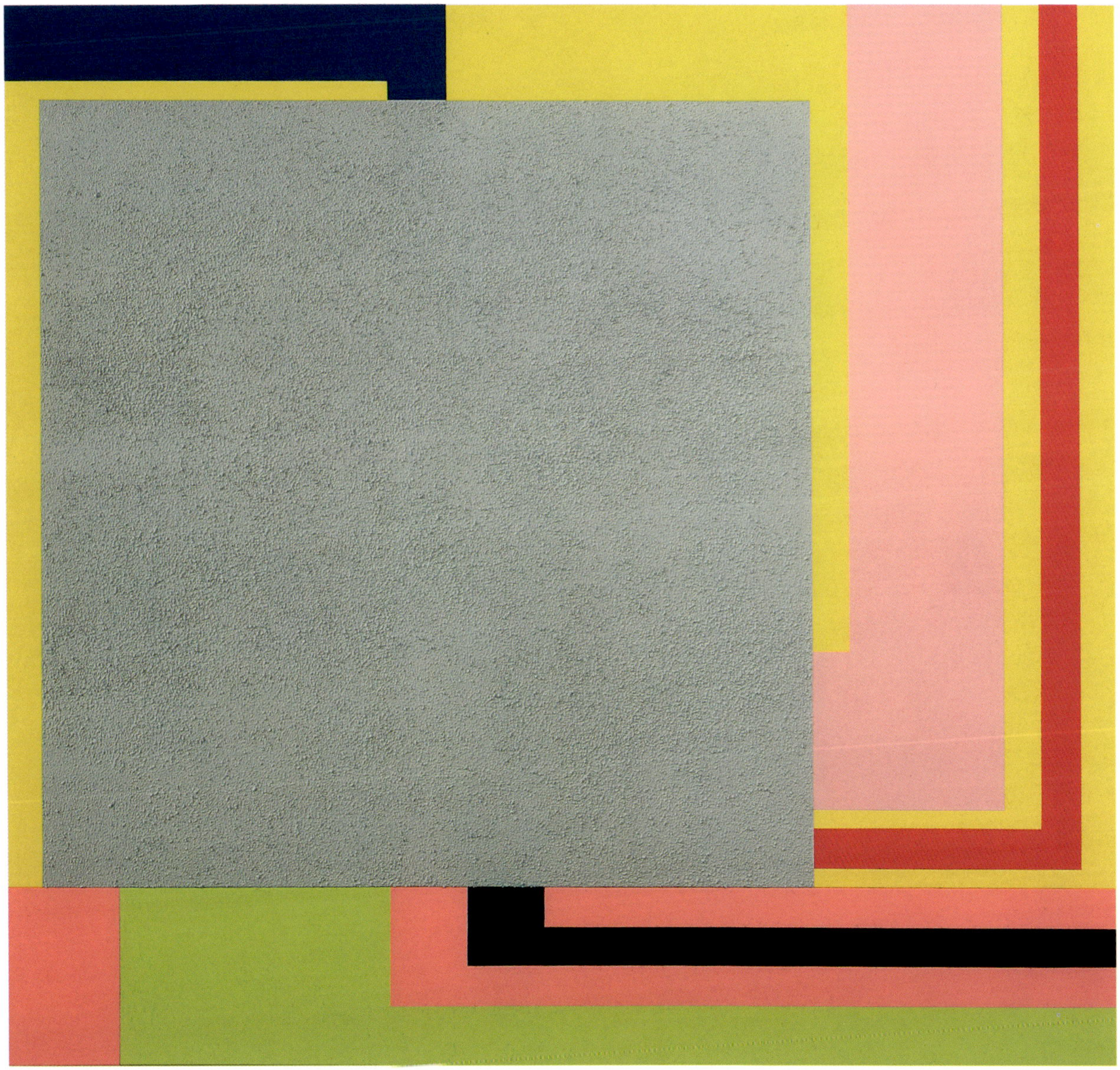

A Dangerous Game, 1993, acrylic, Day-Glo acrylic, and Roll-a-Tex on canvas, 84 5/8 x 90 3/4 inches

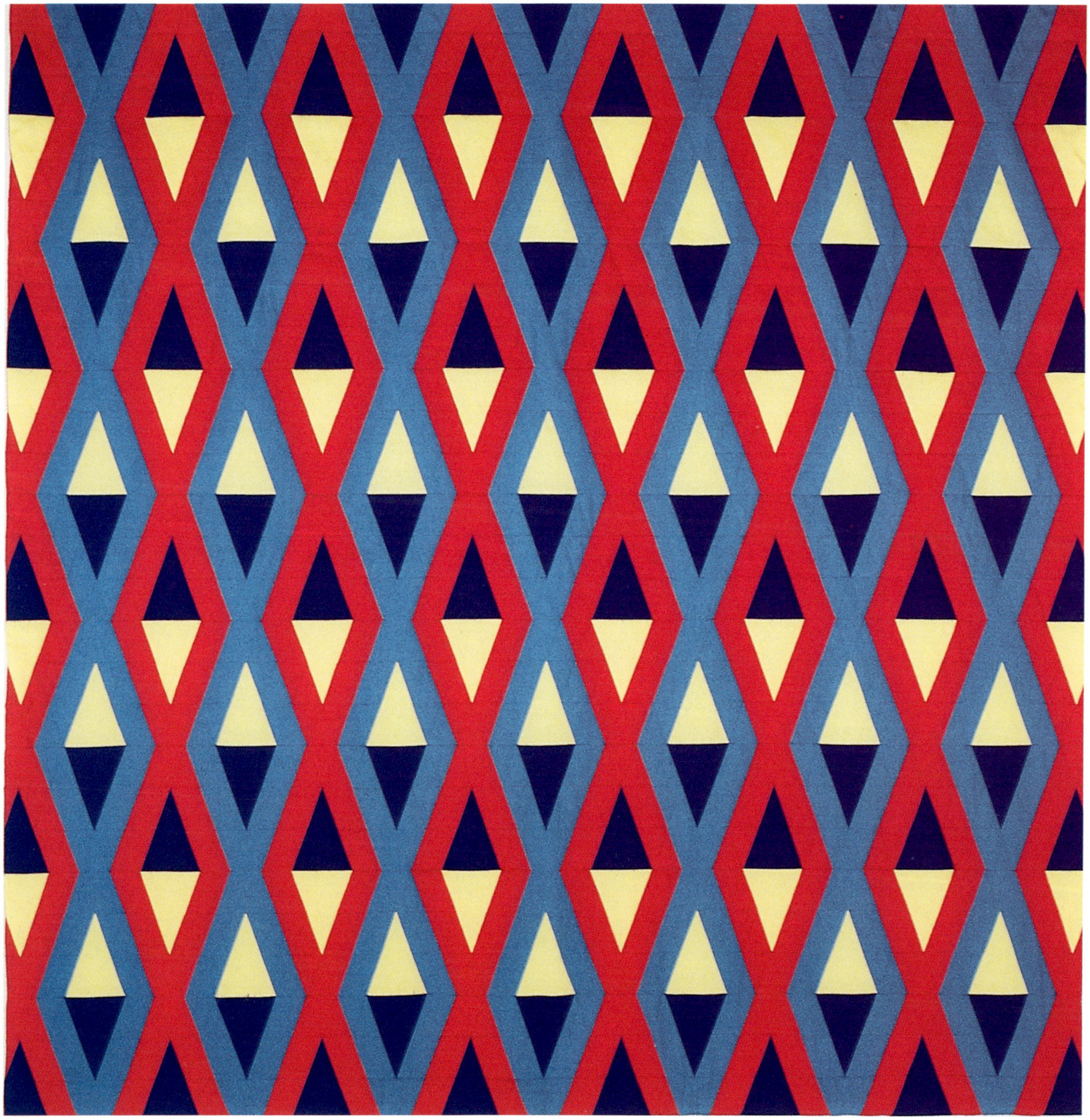

Untitled (fabric wall-hanging), 1993, pieced cotton and cotton-blend quilt top, 76 x 76 inches

jim isermann

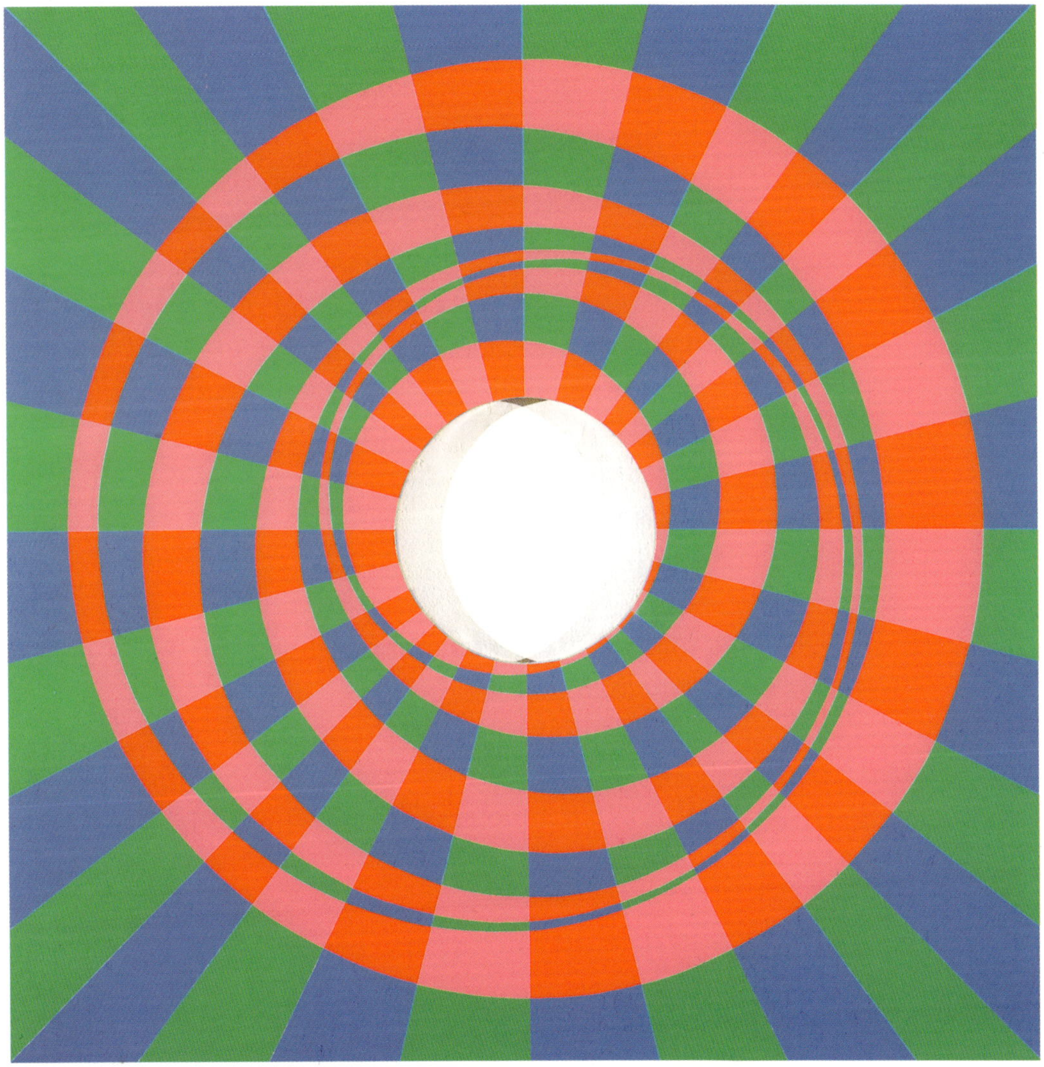

Untitled (hole painting), 1987, enamel on wood, 48 x 48 x 2 inches

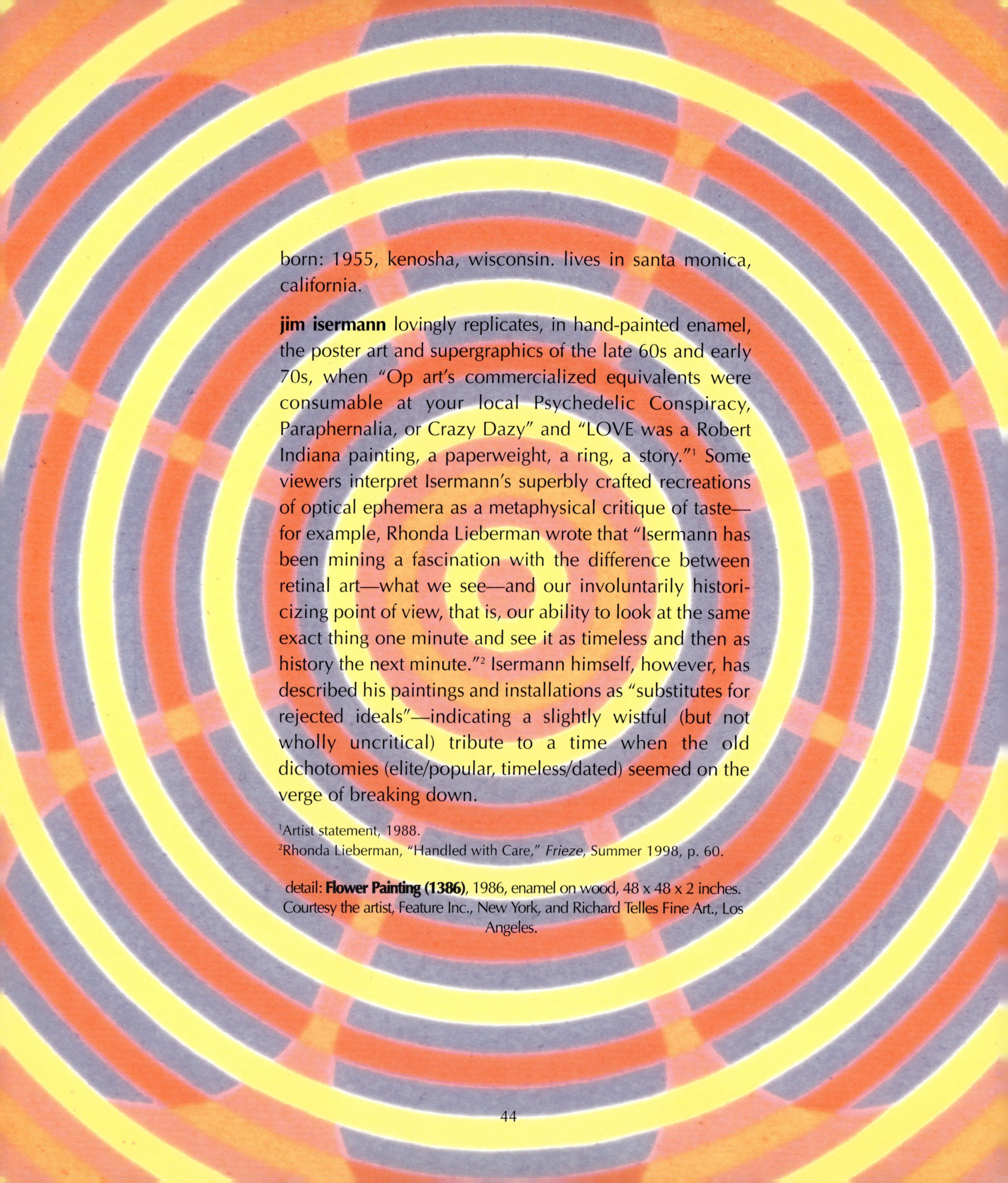

born: 1955, kenosha, wisconsin. lives in santa monica, california.

jim isermann lovingly replicates, in hand-painted enamel, the poster art and supergraphics of the late 60s and early 70s, when "Op art's commercialized equivalents were consumable at your local Psychedelic Conspiracy, Paraphernalia, or Crazy Dazy" and "LOVE was a Robert Indiana painting, a paperweight, a ring, a story."[1] Some viewers interpret Isermann's superbly crafted recreations of optical ephemera as a metaphysical critique of taste—for example, Rhonda Lieberman wrote that "Isermann has been mining a fascination with the difference between retinal art—what we see—and our involuntarily historicizing point of view, that is, our ability to look at the same exact thing one minute and see it as timeless and then as history the next minute."[2] Isermann himself, however, has described his paintings and installations as "substitutes for rejected ideals"—indicating a slightly wistful (but not wholly uncritical) tribute to a time when the old dichotomies (elite/popular, timeless/dated) seemed on the verge of breaking down.

[1]Artist statement, 1988.

[2]Rhonda Lieberman, "Handled with Care," *Frieze*, Summer 1998, p. 60.

detail: **Flower Painting (1386)**, 1986, enamel on wood, 48 x 48 x 2 inches. Courtesy the artist, Feature Inc., New York, and Richard Telles Fine Art., Los Angeles.

born: 1929, matsumoto-shi, naganoken, japan. lives in tokyo.

There was a vase of golden violets. . . and when I looked at them and then looked away they began to cover everything. They were on the drawings I was doing and then I saw they were all over the phone book, and going up the walls and then I saw they covered the doors so that I could not see a way out of the room.[1]

yayoi kusama, a kind of elder statesman for the artists in **post-hypnotic**, has long claimed to be inspired by primal, visionary experience—an oceanic shower of dots permeating her world, like the violets in the above-quoted passage. Unlike the typical space-filling doodling of outsider artists (e. g., Howard Finster's skies full of planetoids), her paintings are rigorous and sophisticated, and her work has continued to grow and change throughout her career. In the 1960s, her weblike configurations of small, painterly marks ("nets") influenced the nascent Minimalist movement, and in the 90s, her intricate patterns of dots, arranged in molecular and tentacle-like clusters, speak to artists interested in process and optical buzz. **Crowd**, for example, combines the outsider's *horror vacui* with an intuitive spatial mathematics recalling Mandelbrot sets and iterative graphics software. A network of shifting, Albersian figure-ground reversals turns a simple yellow-blue color scheme and flat, uninflected paint application into a perpetually dynamic visual field.

[1]Kusama describing an afternoon at home in her late adolescence, "Dot Dot Dot," *Artforum*, February 1997, p. 69.

detail: **Grass A**, acrylic on canvas, 46 x 36 inches
Courtesy Robert Miller Gallery, New York

yayoi kusama

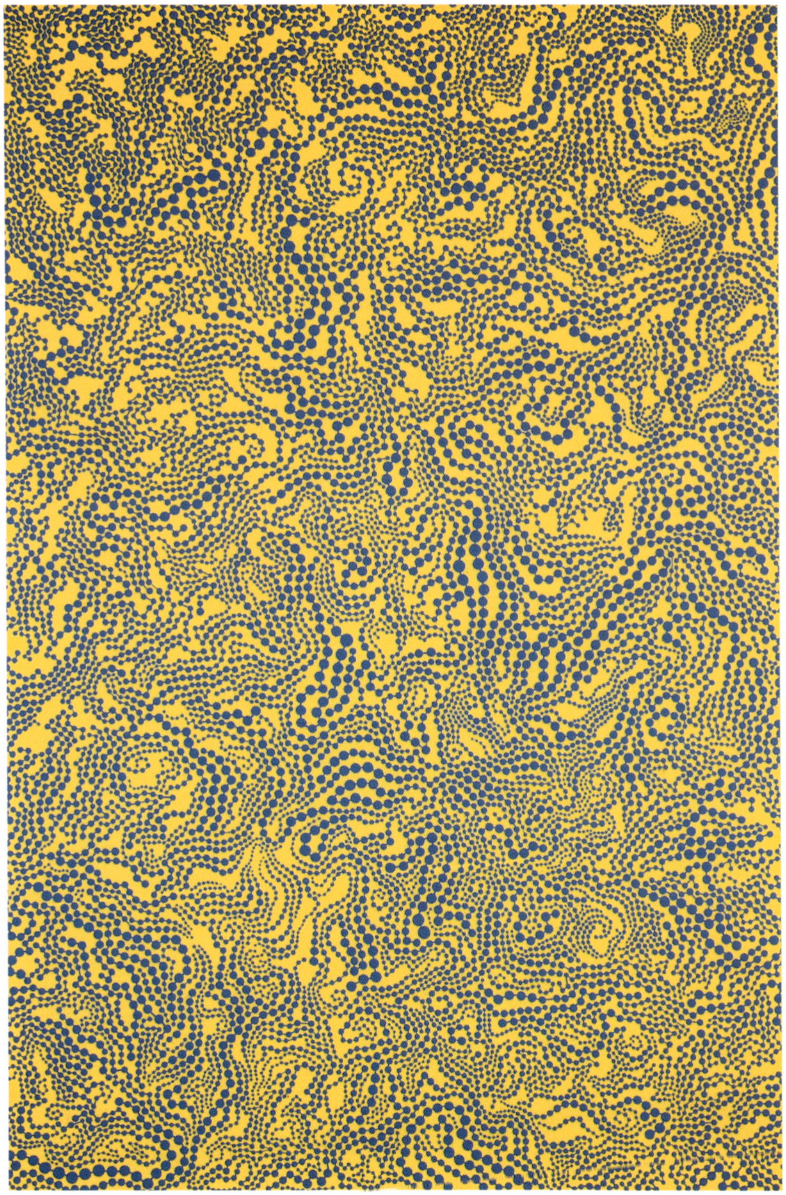

Crowd, 1992, acrylic on canvas, 76 1/4 x 51 3/8 inches
opposite: **Dots Accumulation**, 1995, acrylic on canvas, 115 x 90 1/2 inches

Groovin' on Lemon & Silver, 1996, oil and wax on canvas, 84 x 96 inches

judy ledgerwood

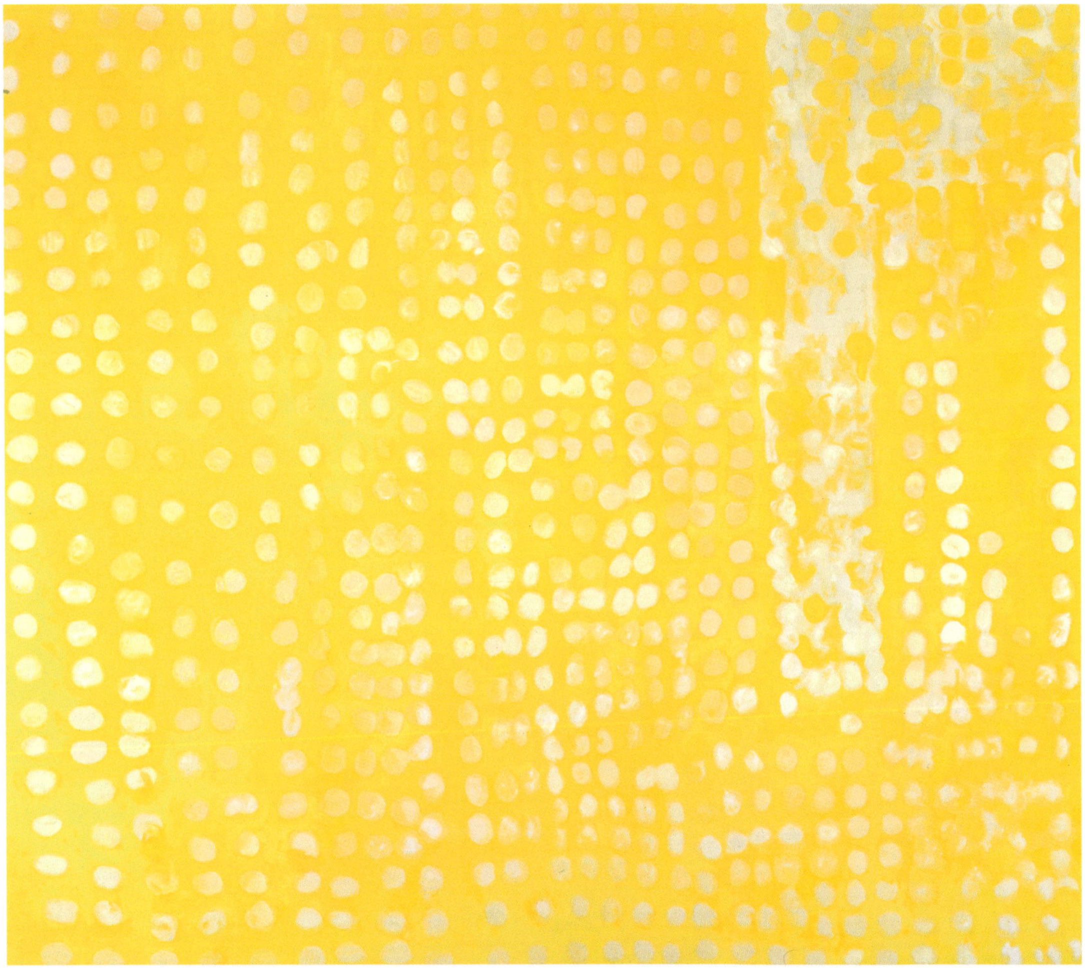

In the Groove, 1996, oil and wax on canvas, 84 x 96 inches

born: 1959, brazil, indiana. lives in oak park, illinois.

In the Abstract Expressionist period, pure color was entwined with notions of transcendence. In Barnett Newman's work, massive planes were meant to invoke ecstatic feeling, while the slow differentiation of virtually identical hues in Ad Reinhardt's black-on-black paintings resembled a zen-like road to enlightenment. As one stares at the vast, engulfing field of yellow flecked with white daubs in **In the Groove**, the "whites" gradually yield up faint tints of purple, pulsing in and out of the surrounding complementary color. Yet in contrast to, say, Rothko's rectangles, which glowed with an immanent, interior light and supposedly existed independent of all external reference, **judy ledgerwood** seems just as concerned with mediation as meditation: her soft brushy orbs resemble out-of-focus Ben Day dots hitting the canvas from some distant projector.

detail: **In the Groove**, 1996, oil and wax on canvas, 84 x 96 inches
Courtesy Feigen Contemporary, New York

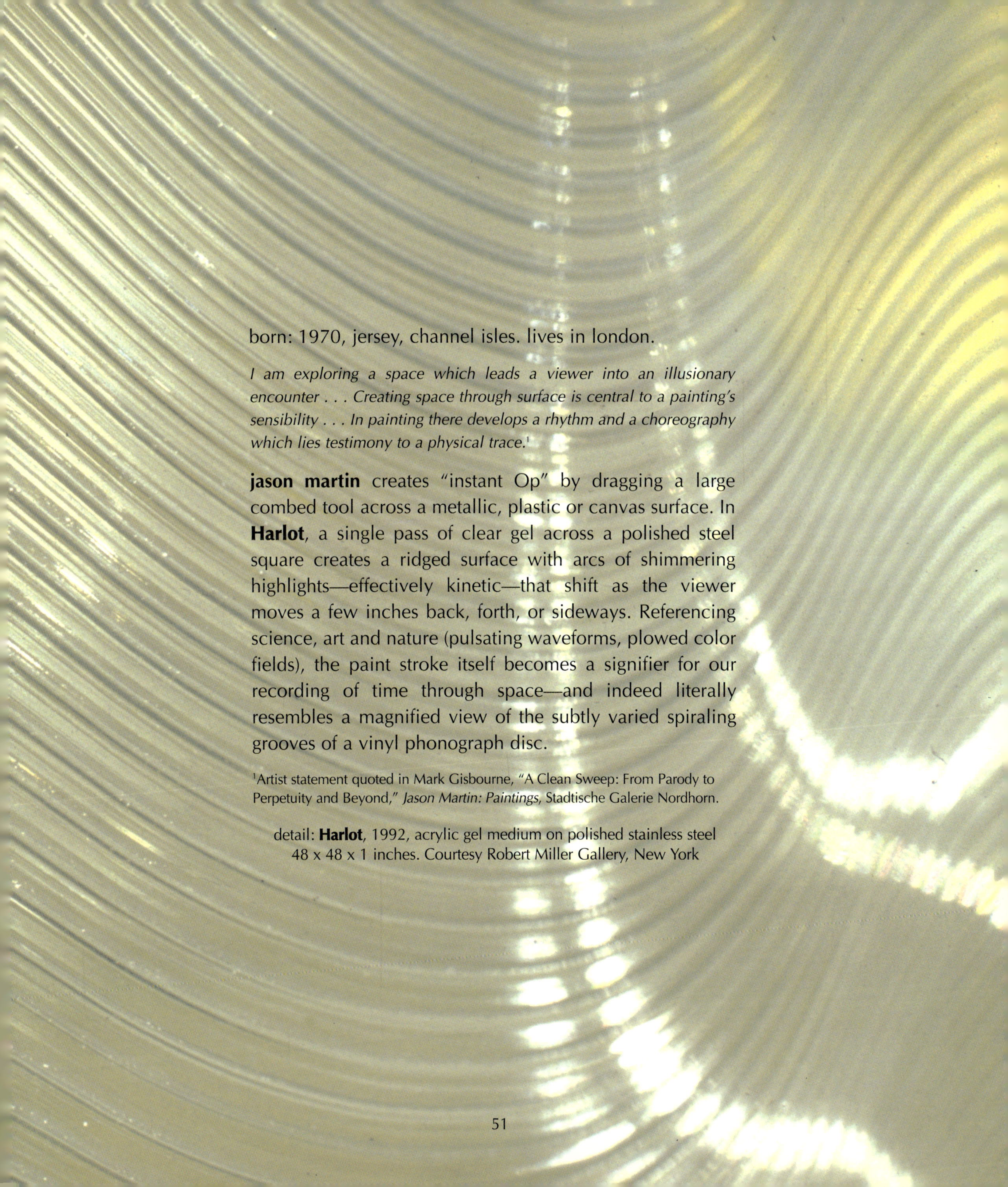

born: 1970, jersey, channel isles. lives in london.

I am exploring a space which leads a viewer into an illusionary encounter . . . Creating space through surface is central to a painting's sensibility . . . In painting there develops a rhythm and a choreography which lies testimony to a physical trace.[1]

jason martin creates "instant Op" by dragging a large combed tool across a metallic, plastic or canvas surface. In **Harlot**, a single pass of clear gel across a polished steel square creates a ridged surface with arcs of shimmering highlights—effectively kinetic—that shift as the viewer moves a few inches back, forth, or sideways. Referencing science, art and nature (pulsating waveforms, plowed color fields), the paint stroke itself becomes a signifier for our recording of time through space—and indeed literally resembles a magnified view of the subtly varied spiraling grooves of a vinyl phonograph disc.

[1] Artist statement quoted in Mark Gisbourne, "A Clean Sweep: From Parody to Perpetuity and Beyond," *Jason Martin: Paintings*, Stadtische Galerie Nordhorn.

detail: **Harlot**, 1992, acrylic gel medium on polished stainless steel
48 x 48 x 1 inches. Courtesy Robert Miller Gallery, New York

jason martin

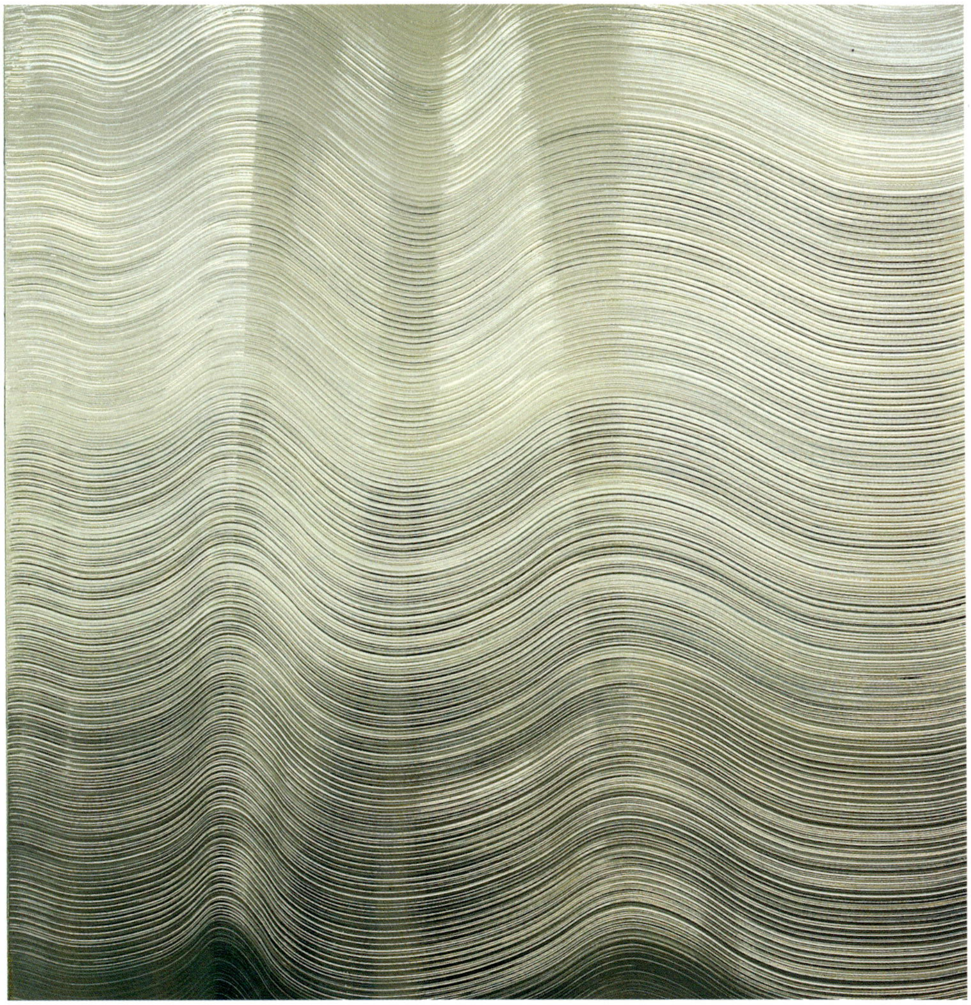

Harlot, 1992, acrylic gel medium on polished stainless steel, 48 x 48 x 1 inches
opposite: **Freeway**, 1997, oil on perspex, 47 1/4 x 47 1/4 inches

tom martinelli

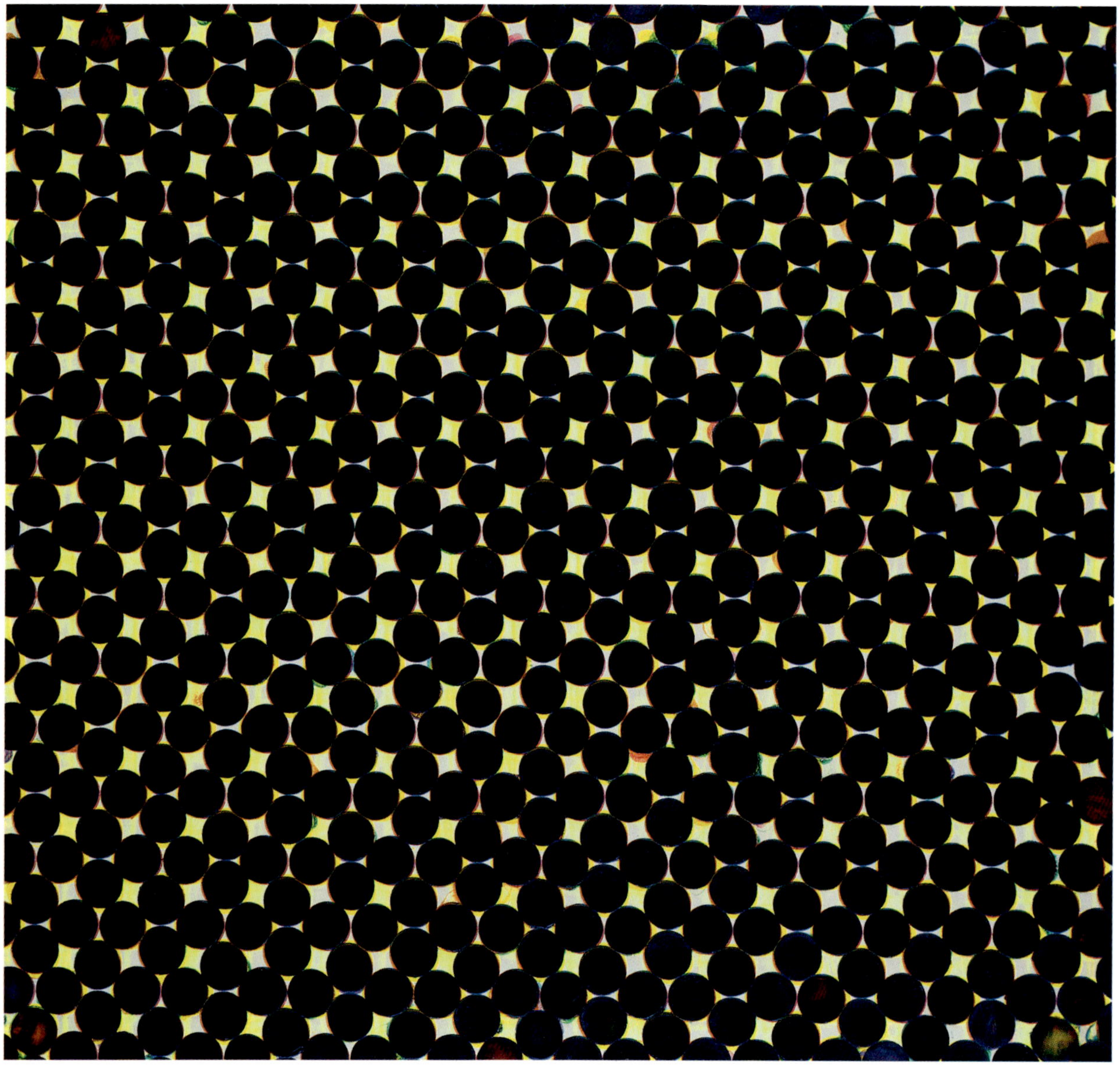

Untitled #9626, 1997, acrylic on canvas, 70 x 76 inches
opposite: **Untitled #9546**, 1995, acrylic on canvas, 76 x 70 inches

born: queens, new york. lives in new york.

Like Roy Lichtenstein, **tom martinelli** has made something of a fetish of the dot, but instead of the simple, single-color Ben Day patterns of 60s comic books, his resemble the dense four-color tonalities of high-end magazines—blown up and purged of imagistic reference. As Owen Drolet has written, "In these paintings every aspect of the process is decipherable; a white ground is covered with 'black' dots that are in fact built by layers of primary and secondary colors. As the stencil used to create each layer shifts slightly with each application, pure color is left exposed at the perimeter of the dots. As straightforward a process as this is, it creates a complex visual situation in which micro and macro relations within each painting are put into a state of continual flux. The optical effects, which at times create an entirely ambiguous space, are the result of the regularity of the dots and the irregularity of the colors that seep from them."[1]

[1]Owen Drolet, "Tom Martinelli." Catalogue essay, Bill Maynes Contemporary Art, New York, 1995.

detail: **Untitled #9601**, 1996, acrylic on canvas, 76 x 70 inches
Courtesy the artist

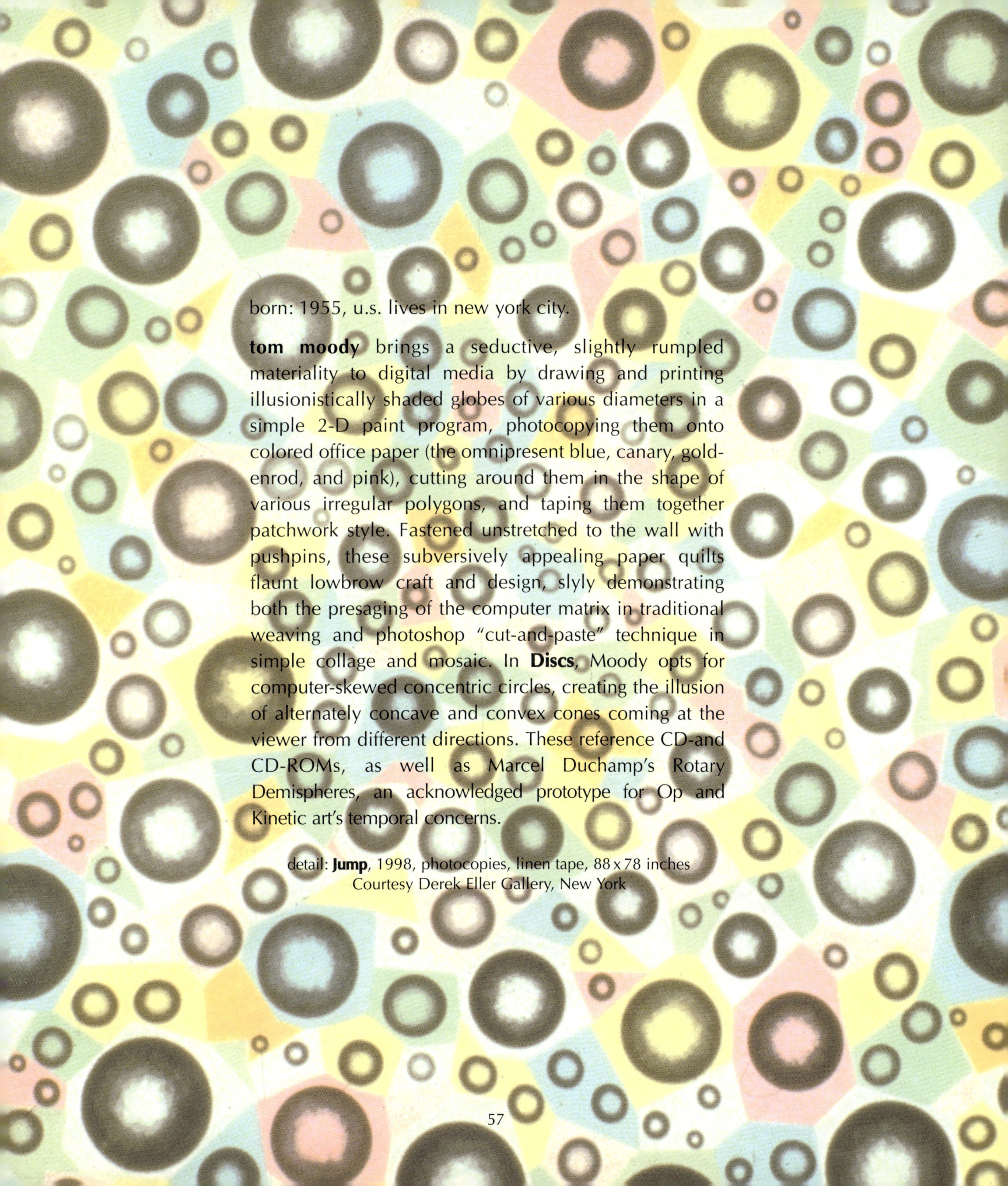

born: 1955, u.s. lives in new york city.

tom moody brings a seductive, slightly rumpled materiality to digital media by drawing and printing illusionistically shaded globes of various diameters in a simple 2-D paint program, photocopying them onto colored office paper (the omnipresent blue, canary, goldenrod, and pink), cutting around them in the shape of various irregular polygons, and taping them together patchwork style. Fastened unstretched to the wall with pushpins, these subversively appealing paper quilts flaunt lowbrow craft and design, slyly demonstrating both the presaging of the computer matrix in traditional weaving and photoshop "cut-and-paste" technique in simple collage and mosaic. In **Discs**, Moody opts for computer-skewed concentric circles, creating the illusion of alternately concave and convex cones coming at the viewer from different directions. These reference CD-and CD-ROMs, as well as Marcel Duchamp's Rotary Demispheres, an acknowledged prototype for Op and Kinetic art's temporal concerns.

detail: **Jump**, 1998, photocopies, linen tape, 88 x 78 inches
Courtesy Derek Eller Gallery, New York

tom moody

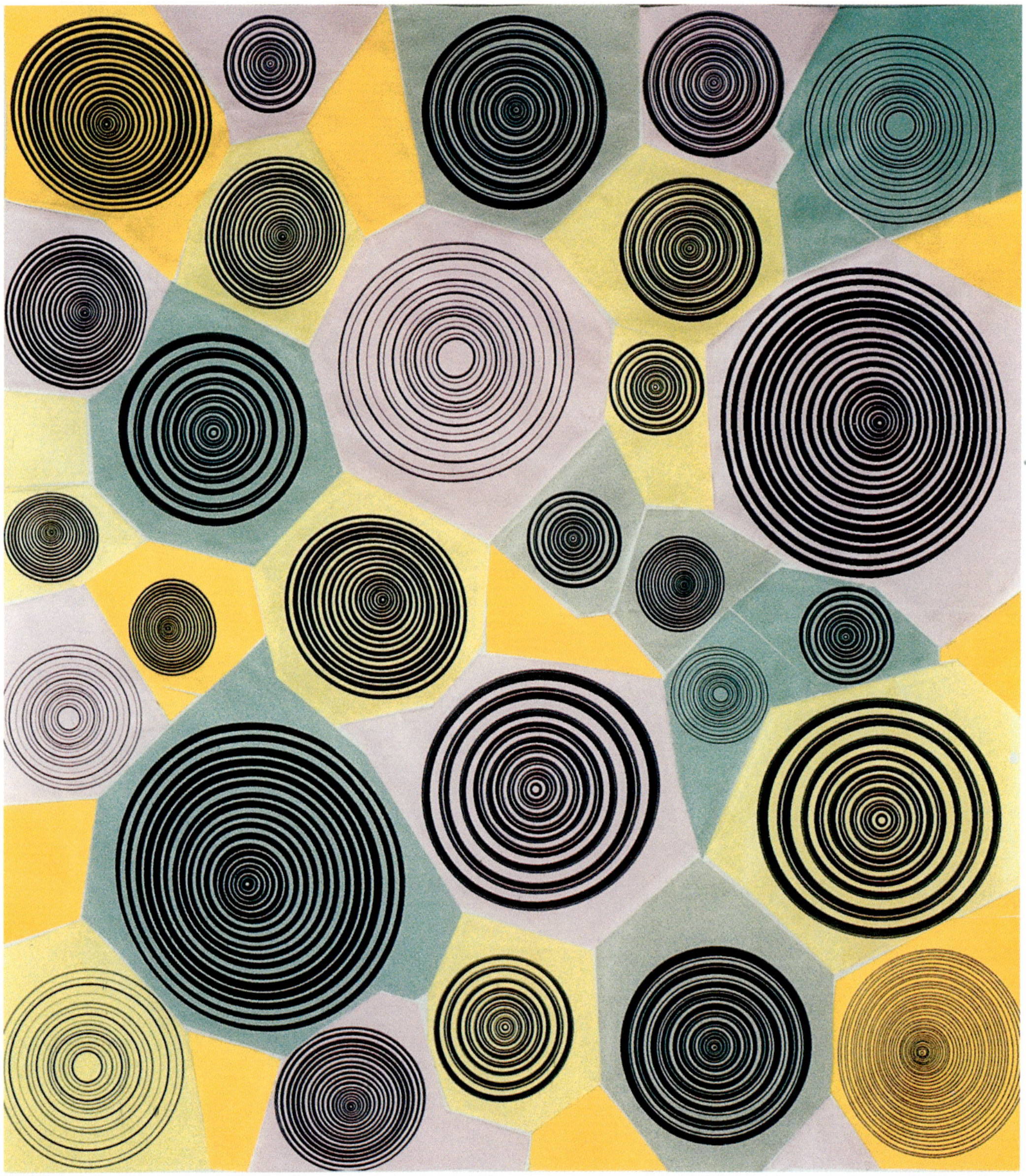

Discs, 1998, photocopies, linen tape, 29 1/2 x 27 inches
opposite: **Greater**, 1997, photocopies, linen tape, 88 x 78 inches

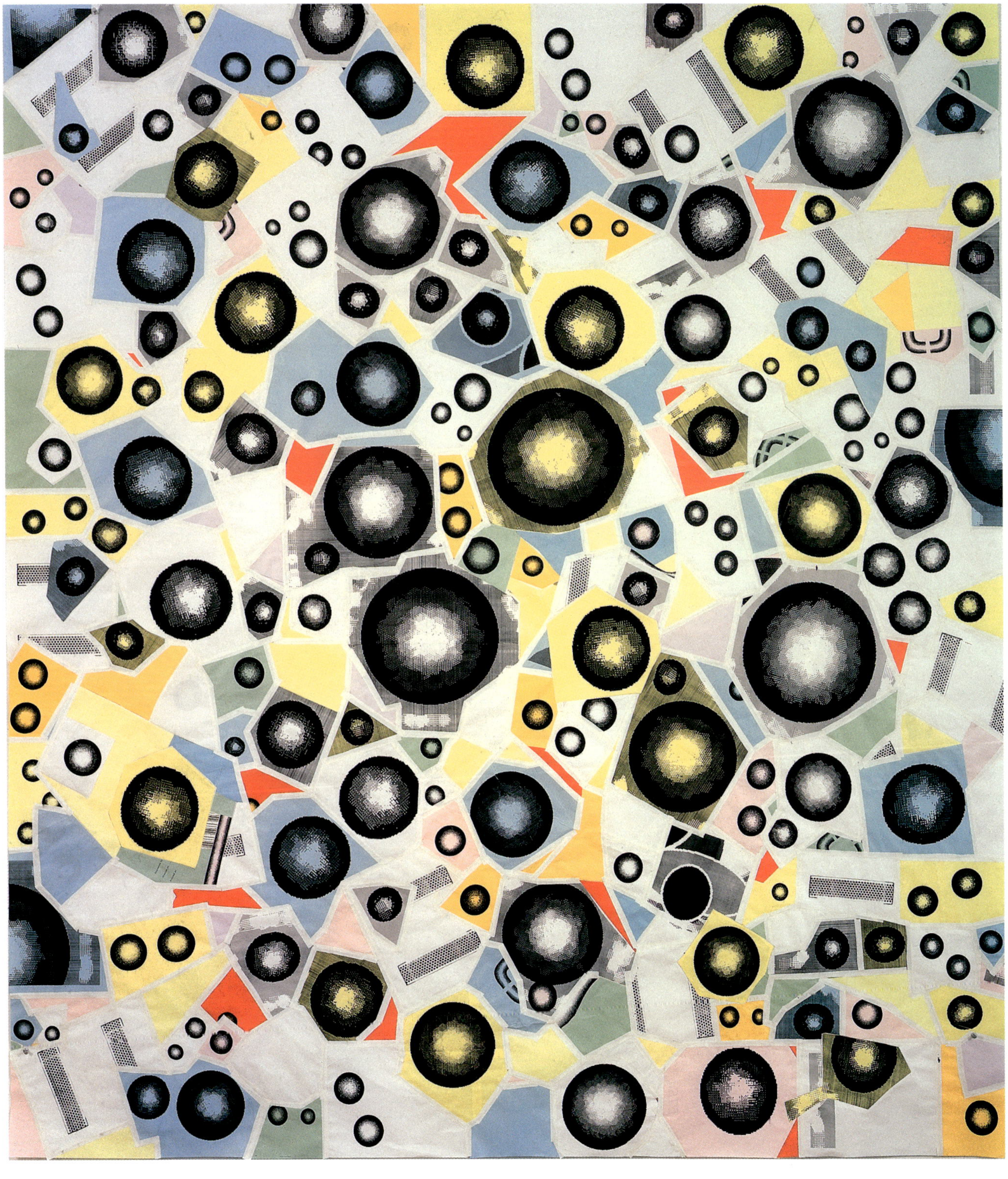

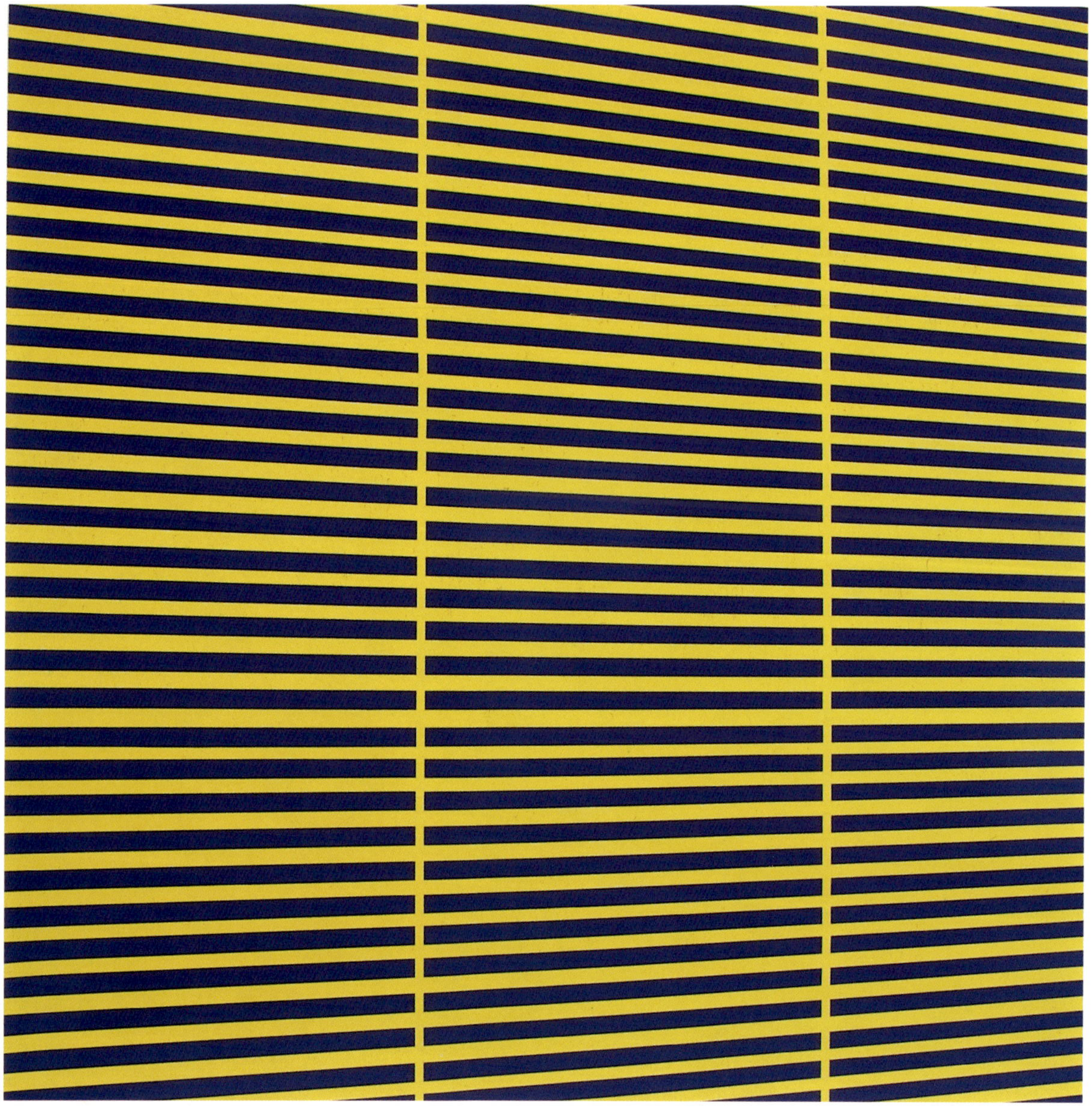

Horizontal Blinds, 1997, gloss household paint on canvas, 84 x 84 inches

sarah morris

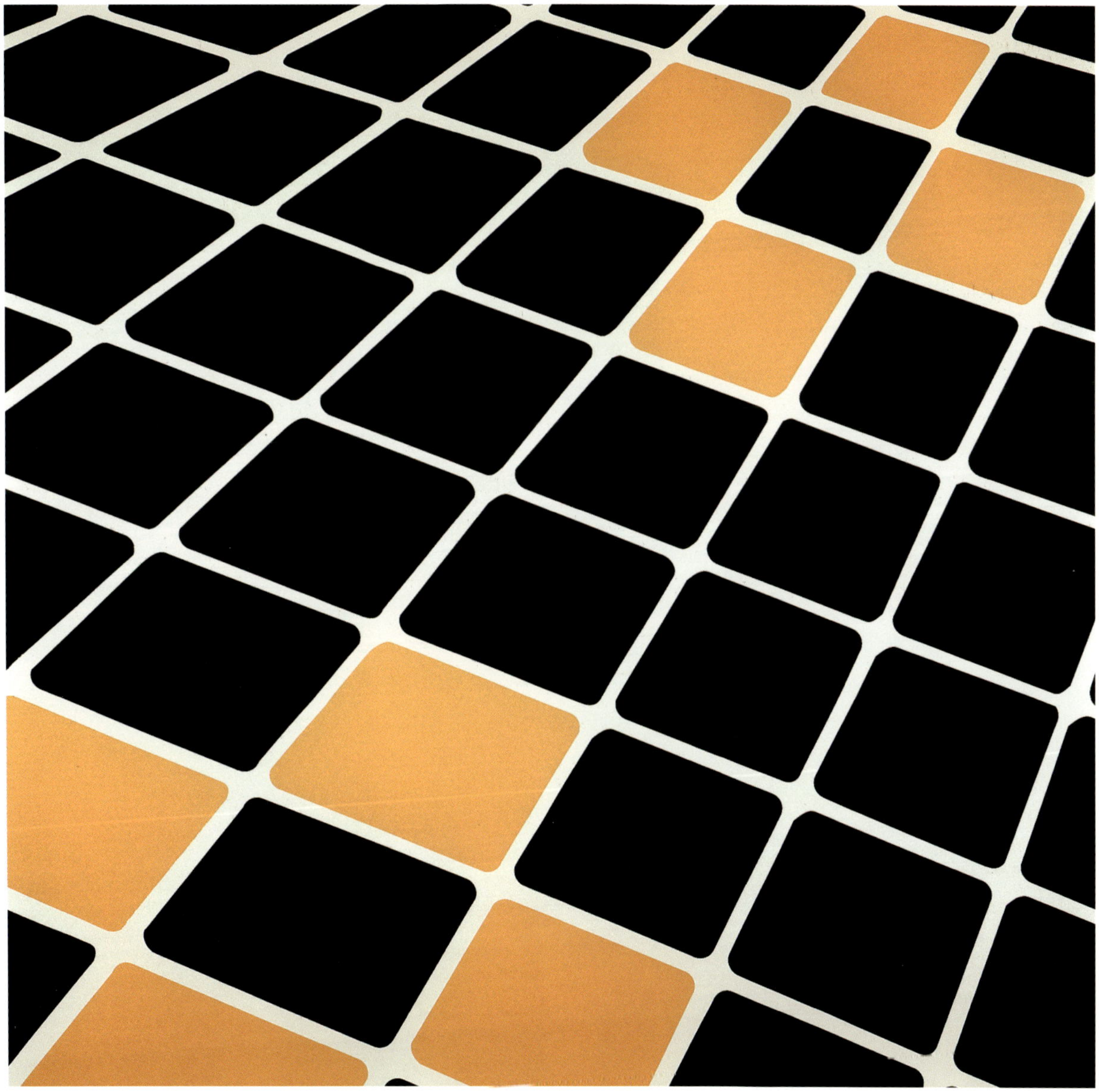

Bathroom Floor (Las Vegas), 1997, gloss household paint on canvas, 72 x 72 inches

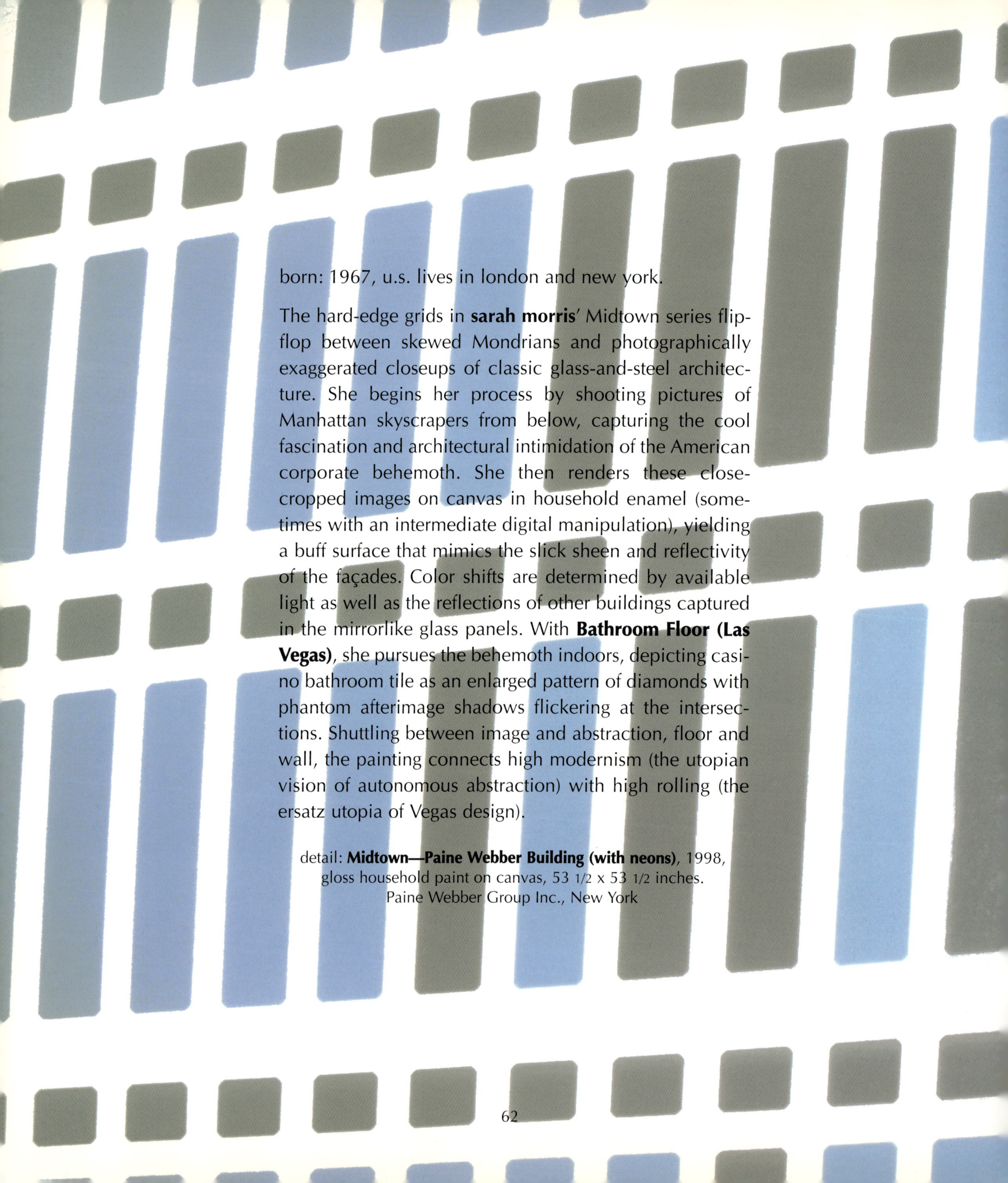

born: 1967, u.s. lives in london and new york.

The hard-edge grids in **sarah morris**' Midtown series flip-flop between skewed Mondrians and photographically exaggerated closeups of classic glass-and-steel architecture. She begins her process by shooting pictures of Manhattan skyscrapers from below, capturing the cool fascination and architectural intimidation of the American corporate behemoth. She then renders these close-cropped images on canvas in household enamel (sometimes with an intermediate digital manipulation), yielding a buff surface that mimics the slick sheen and reflectivity of the façades. Color shifts are determined by available light as well as the reflections of other buildings captured in the mirrorlike glass panels. With **Bathroom Floor (Las Vegas)**, she pursues the behemoth indoors, depicting casino bathroom tile as an enlarged pattern of diamonds with phantom afterimage shadows flickering at the intersections. Shuttling between image and abstraction, floor and wall, the painting connects high modernism (the utopian vision of autonomous abstraction) with high rolling (the ersatz utopia of Vegas design).

detail: **Midtown—Paine Webber Building (with neons)**, 1998,
gloss household paint on canvas, 53 1/2 x 53 1/2 inches.
Paine Webber Group Inc., New York

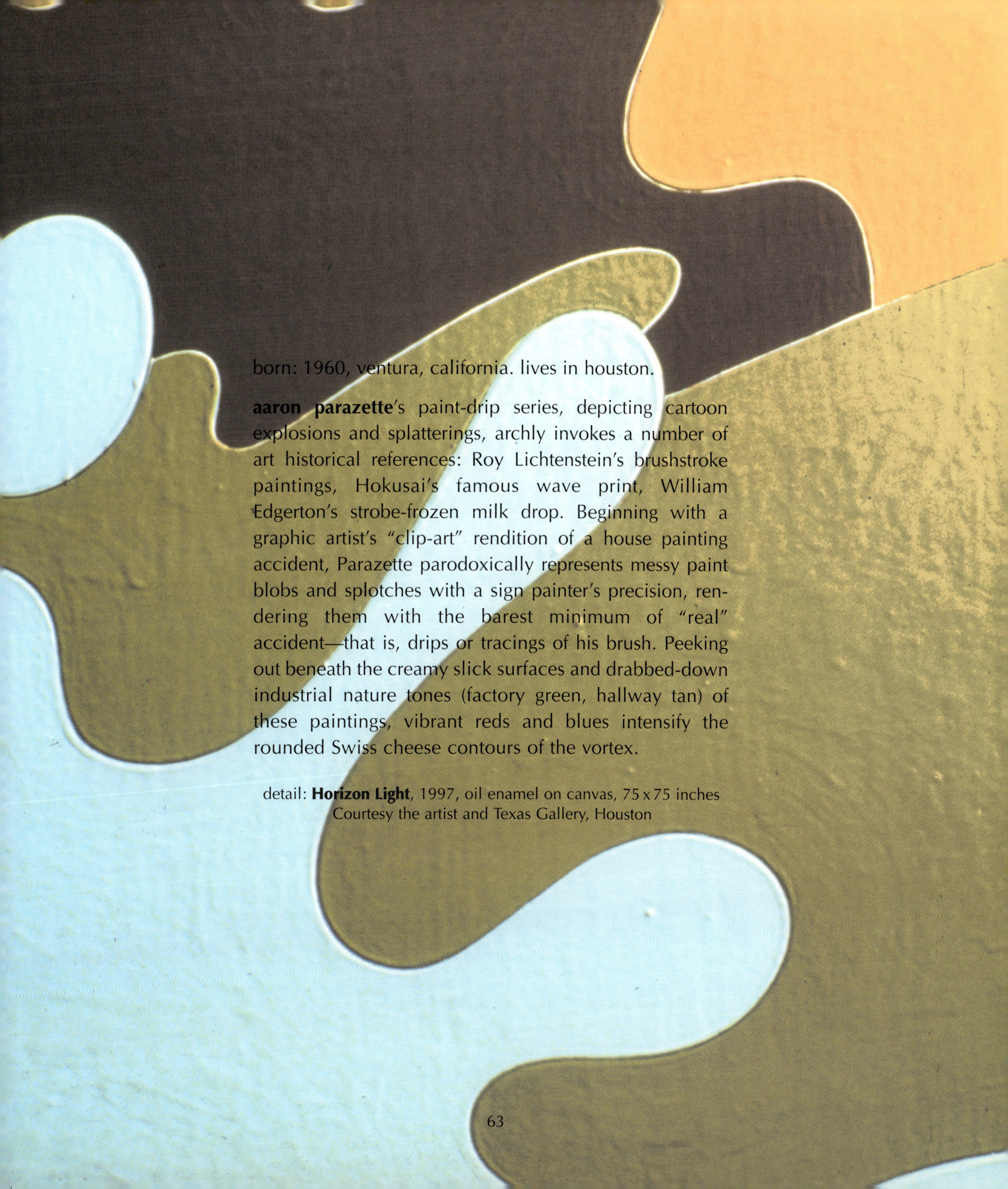

born: 1960, ventura, california. lives in houston.

aaron parazette's paint-drip series, depicting cartoon explosions and splatterings, archly invokes a number of art historical references: Roy Lichtenstein's brushstroke paintings, Hokusai's famous wave print, William Edgerton's strobe-frozen milk drop. Beginning with a graphic artist's "clip-art" rendition of a house painting accident, Parazette parodoxically represents messy paint blobs and splotches with a sign painter's precision, rendering them with the barest minimum of "real" accident—that is, drips or tracings of his brush. Peeking out beneath the creamy slick surfaces and drabbed-down industrial nature tones (factory green, hallway tan) of these paintings, vibrant reds and blues intensify the rounded Swiss cheese contours of the vortex.

detail: **Horizon Light**, 1997, oil enamel on canvas, 75 x 75 inches
Courtesy the artist and Texas Gallery, Houston

aaron
parazette

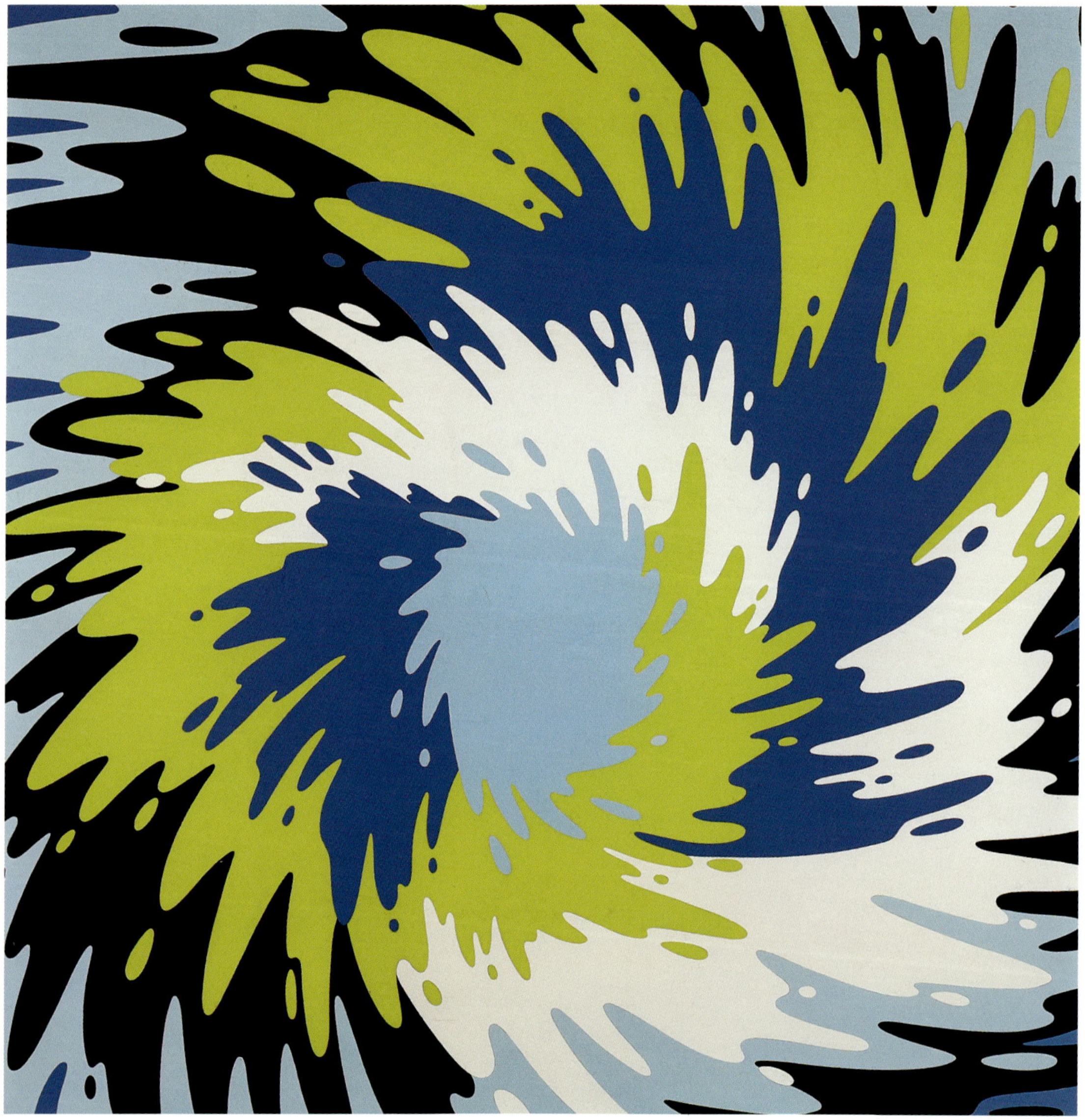

February, 1997, oil enamel on canvas, 75 x 75 inches

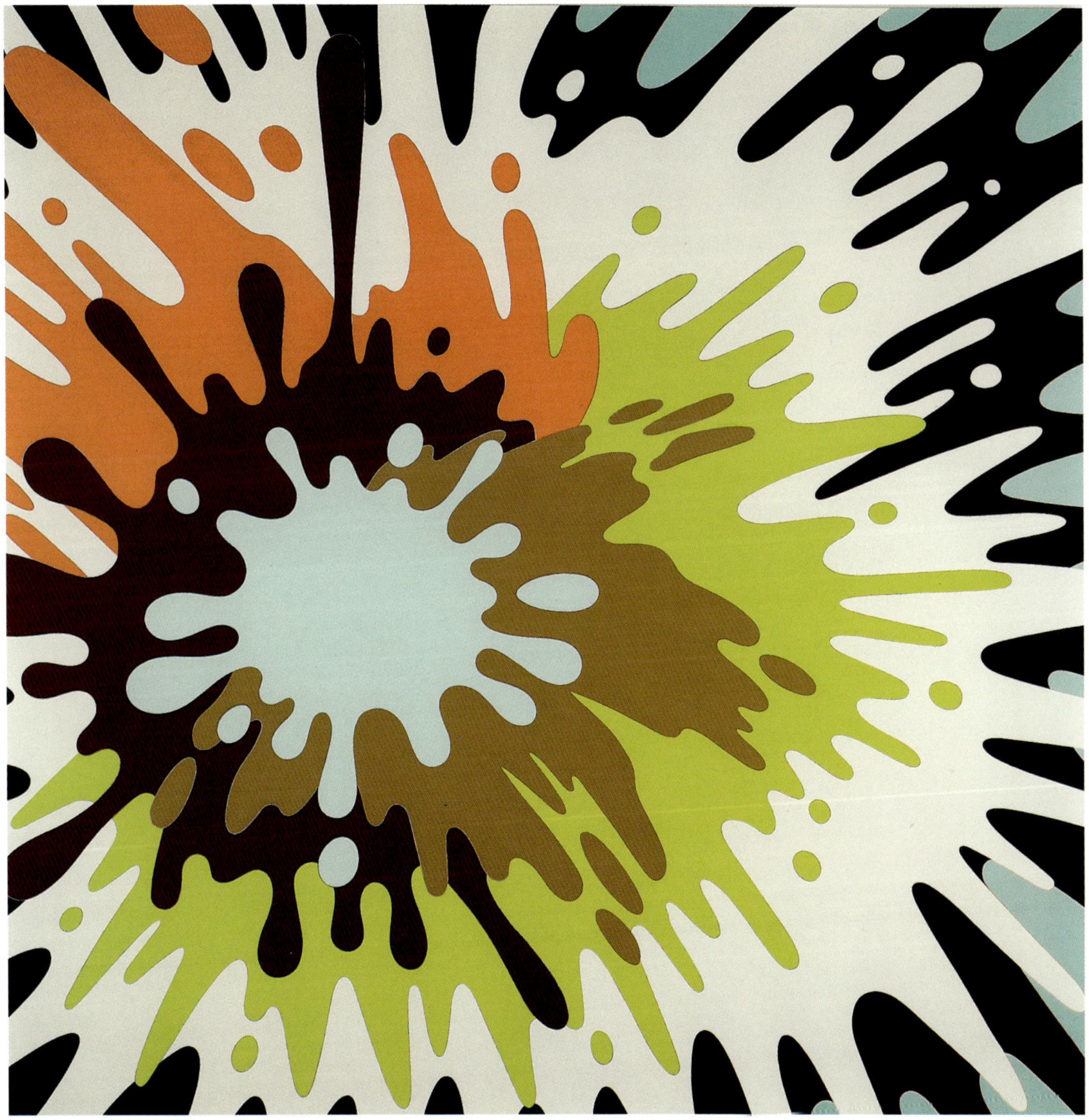

Horizon Light, 1997, oil enamel on canvas, 75 x 75 inches

bruce pearson

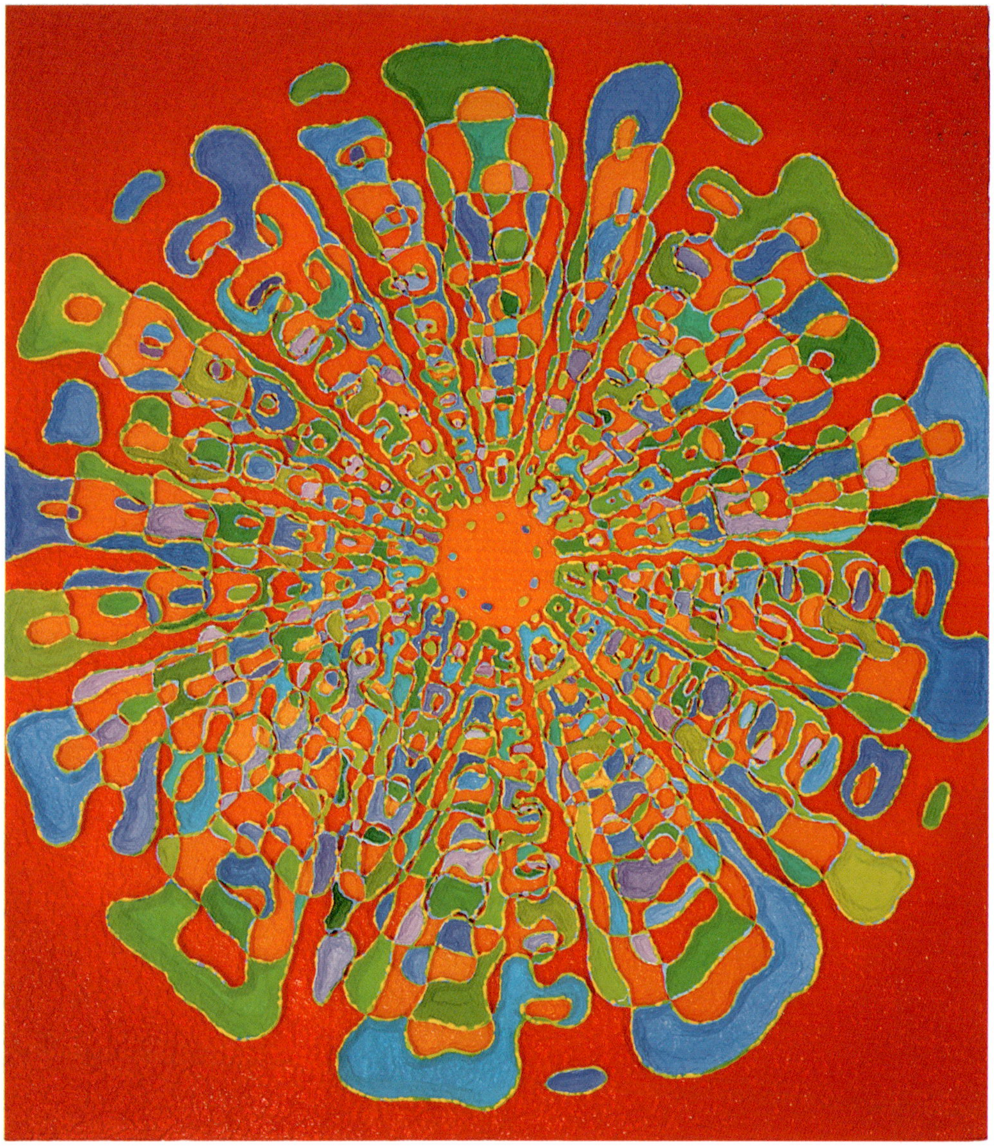

Die of Pleasure, 1998, acrylic on Styrofoam, 82 x 72 inches
opposite: **Wanna Be Happy Be Happy**, 1995, oil and acrylic on Styrofoam, 96 x 71 inches

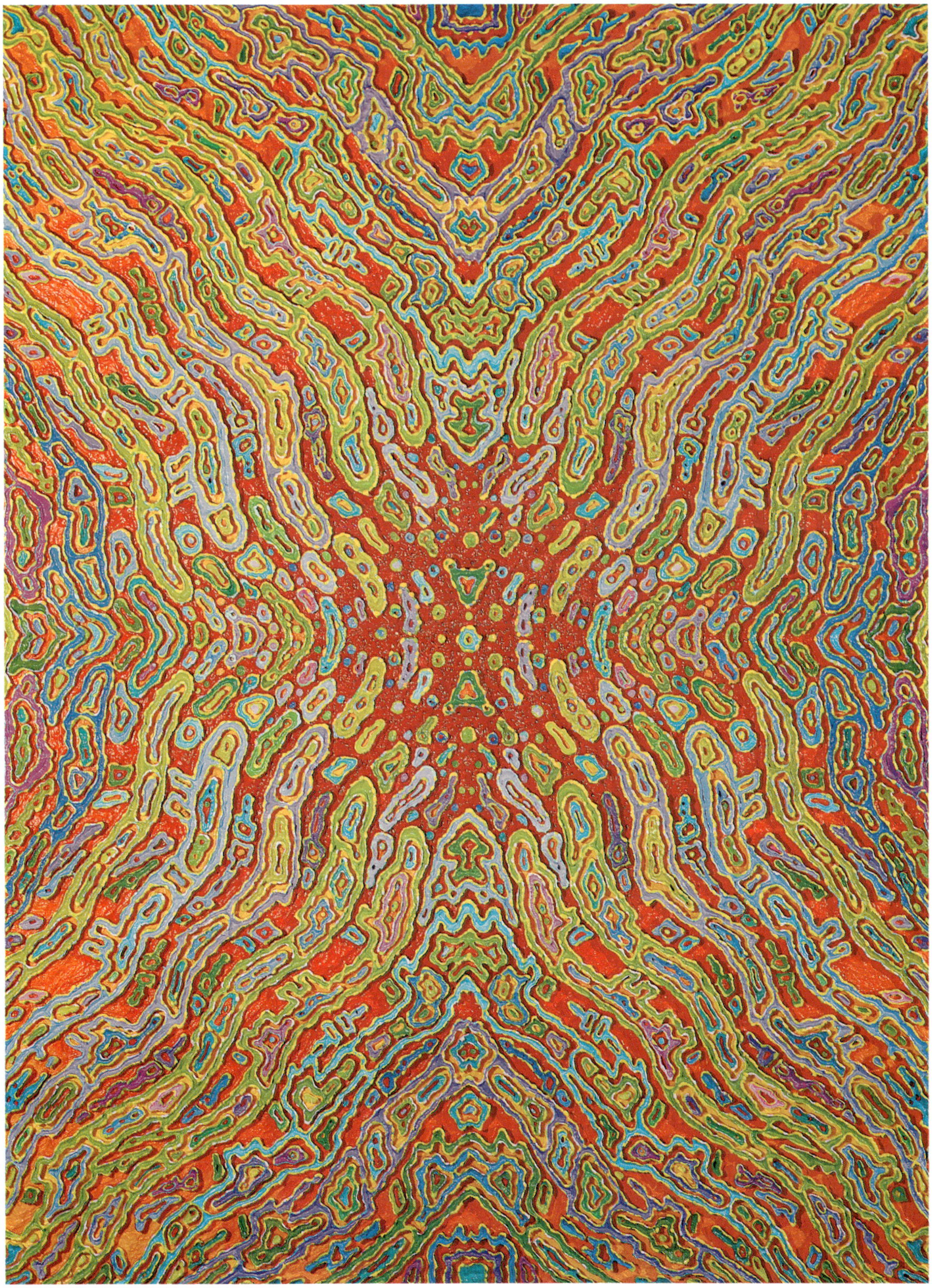

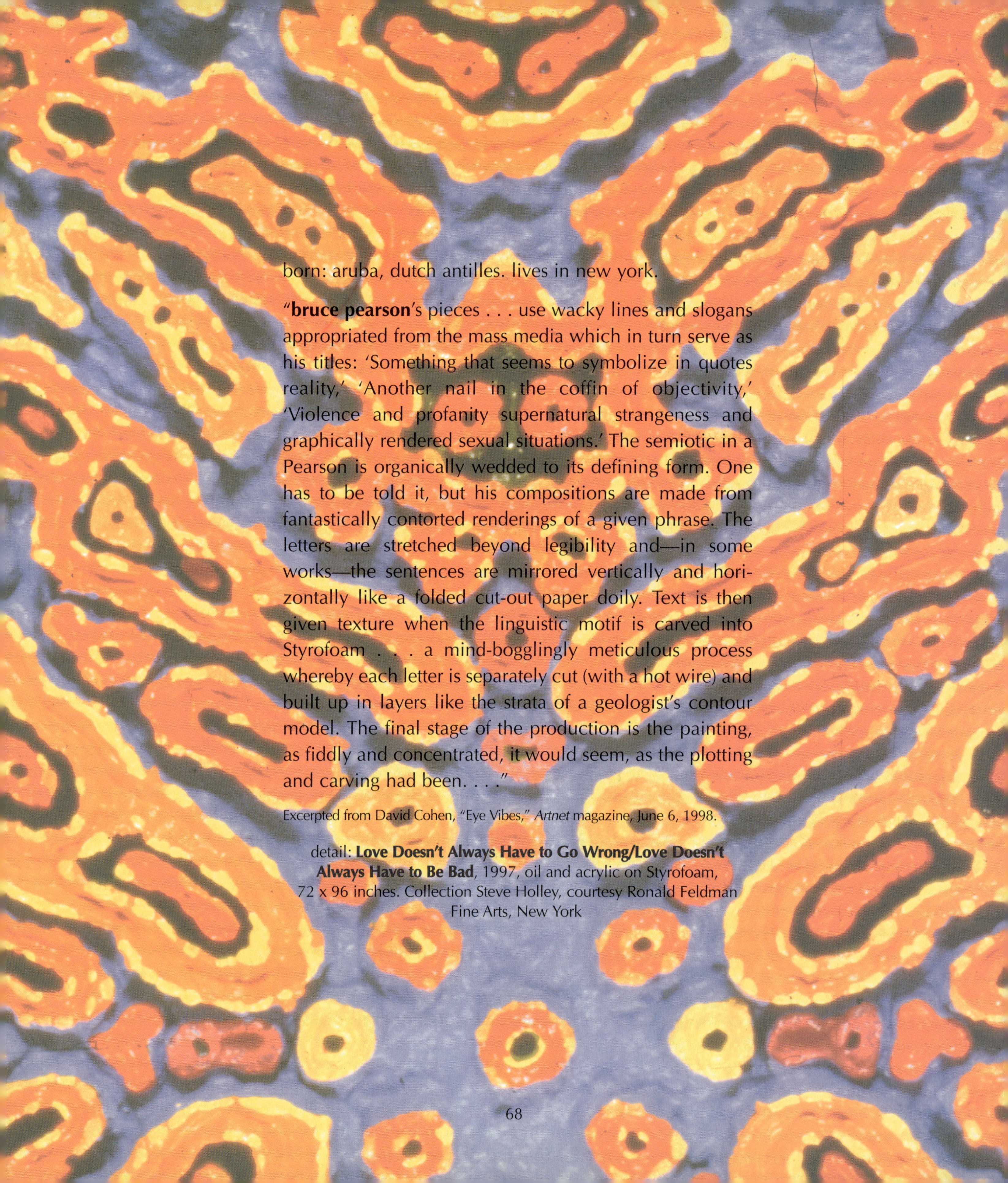

born: aruba, dutch antilles. lives in new york.

"**bruce pearson**'s pieces . . . use wacky lines and slogans appropriated from the mass media which in turn serve as his titles: 'Something that seems to symbolize in quotes reality,' 'Another nail in the coffin of objectivity,' 'Violence and profanity supernatural strangeness and graphically rendered sexual situations.' The semiotic in a Pearson is organically wedded to its defining form. One has to be told it, but his compositions are made from fantastically contorted renderings of a given phrase. The letters are stretched beyond legibility and—in some works—the sentences are mirrored vertically and horizontally like a folded cut-out paper doily. Text is then given texture when the linguistic motif is carved into Styrofoam . . . a mind-bogglingly meticulous process whereby each letter is separately cut (with a hot wire) and built up in layers like the strata of a geologist's contour model. The final stage of the production is the painting, as fiddly and concentrated, it would seem, as the plotting and carving had been. . . ."

Excerpted from David Cohen, "Eye Vibes," *Artnet* magazine, June 6, 1998.

detail: **Love Doesn't Always Have to Go Wrong/Love Doesn't Always Have to Be Bad**, 1997, oil and acrylic on Styrofoam, 72 x 96 inches. Collection Steve Holley, courtesy Ronald Feldman Fine Arts, New York

born: 1950, wilmington, delaware. lives in new york.

Although better known for the pulp-novel cover inspired paintings of detectives and swooning women in negligées he showed at Metro Pictures in the early 1980s, **walter robinson** made a brief but powerful foray into abstraction with his spin art paintings, which reframed New York School painting in the guise of boardwalk art. Unlike Damien Hirst, who exploits this 60s craft gimmick with little stylistic variety, Robinson really used it as a medium, exploring in a highly controlled fashion the rather amazing things that can happen when paint is dropped on a rapidly-spinning horizontal surface. Rhythmically applied drips become a series of seductive, concentric rings; water and oil resist techniques result in intensely optical, quasi-photographic "gestures" à la Gerhard Richter. Installed in series, these paintings form their own sly commentary on 50s, 60s, and even 80s painting; including postmodern "quotations of Jasper Johns' targets, Adolph Gottlieb's bursts, Kenneth Noland's bulls-eyes, and Jack Goldstein's solar systems."[1]

[1] Carlo McCormick, "pOPTOMETRY," *Artforum*, November 1985, p. 90.

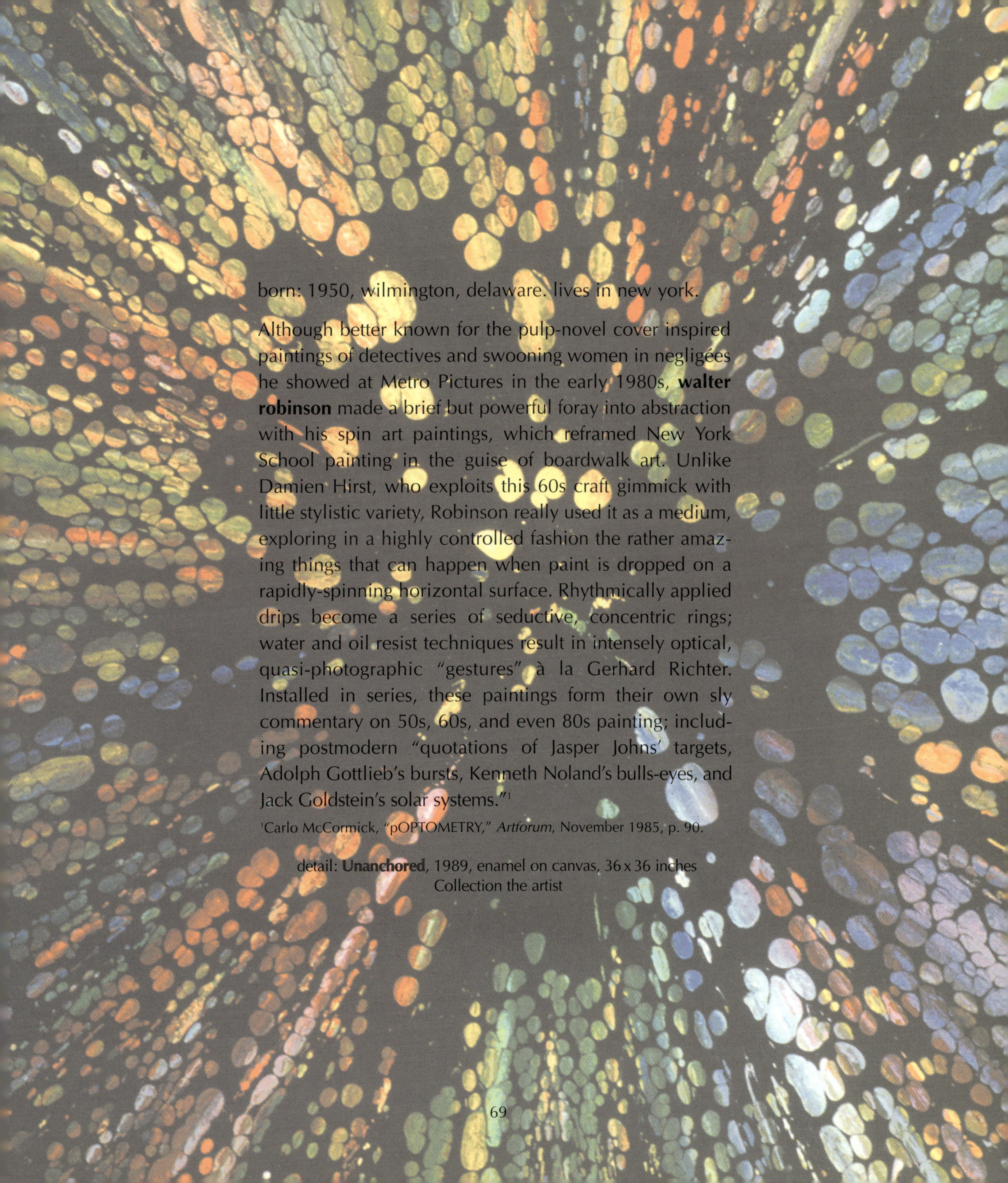

detail: **Unanchored**, 1989, enamel on canvas, 36 x 36 inches
Collection the artist

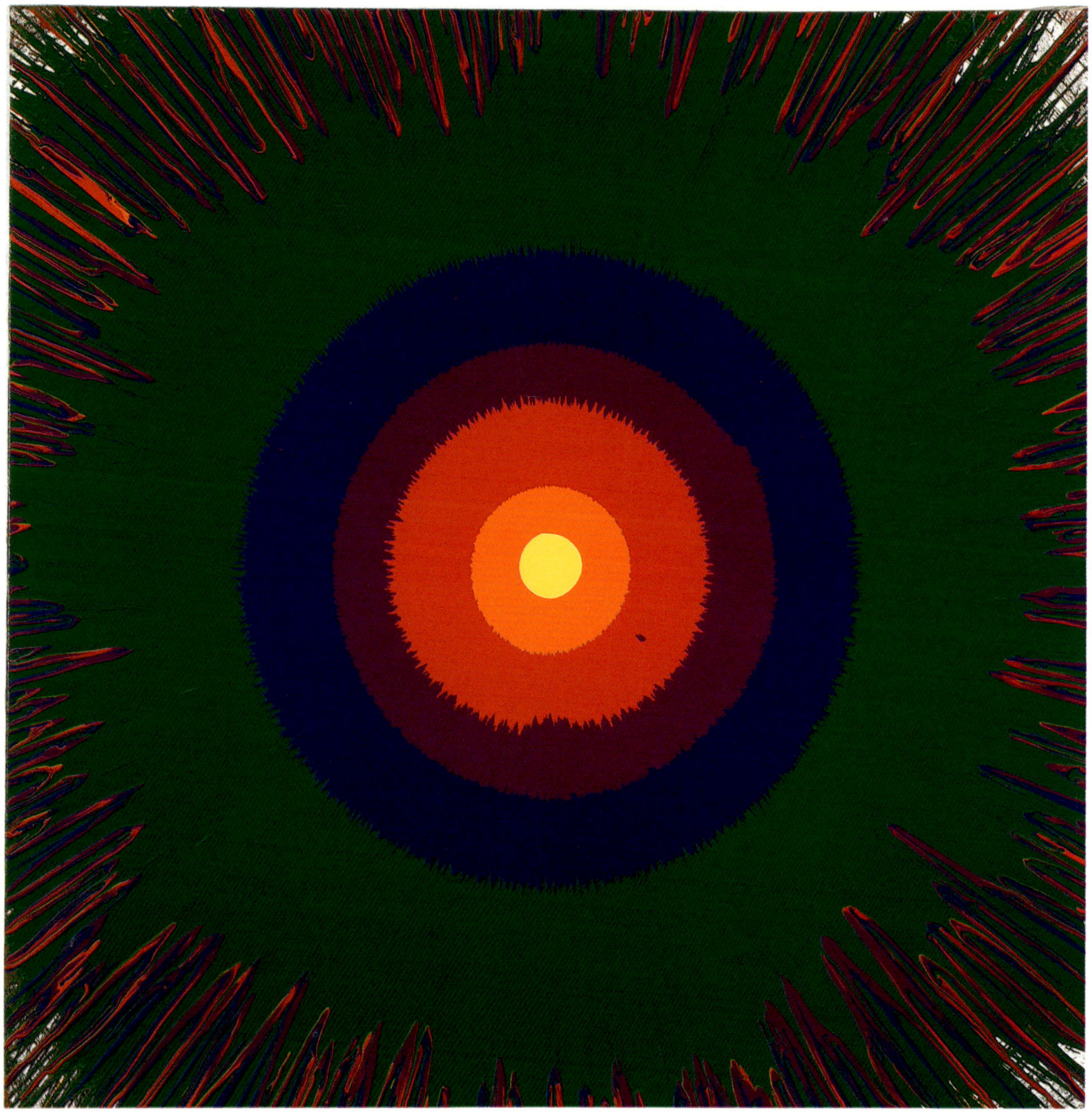

Green Velvet, 1986, oil enamel on canvas, 36 x 36 inches

walter robinson

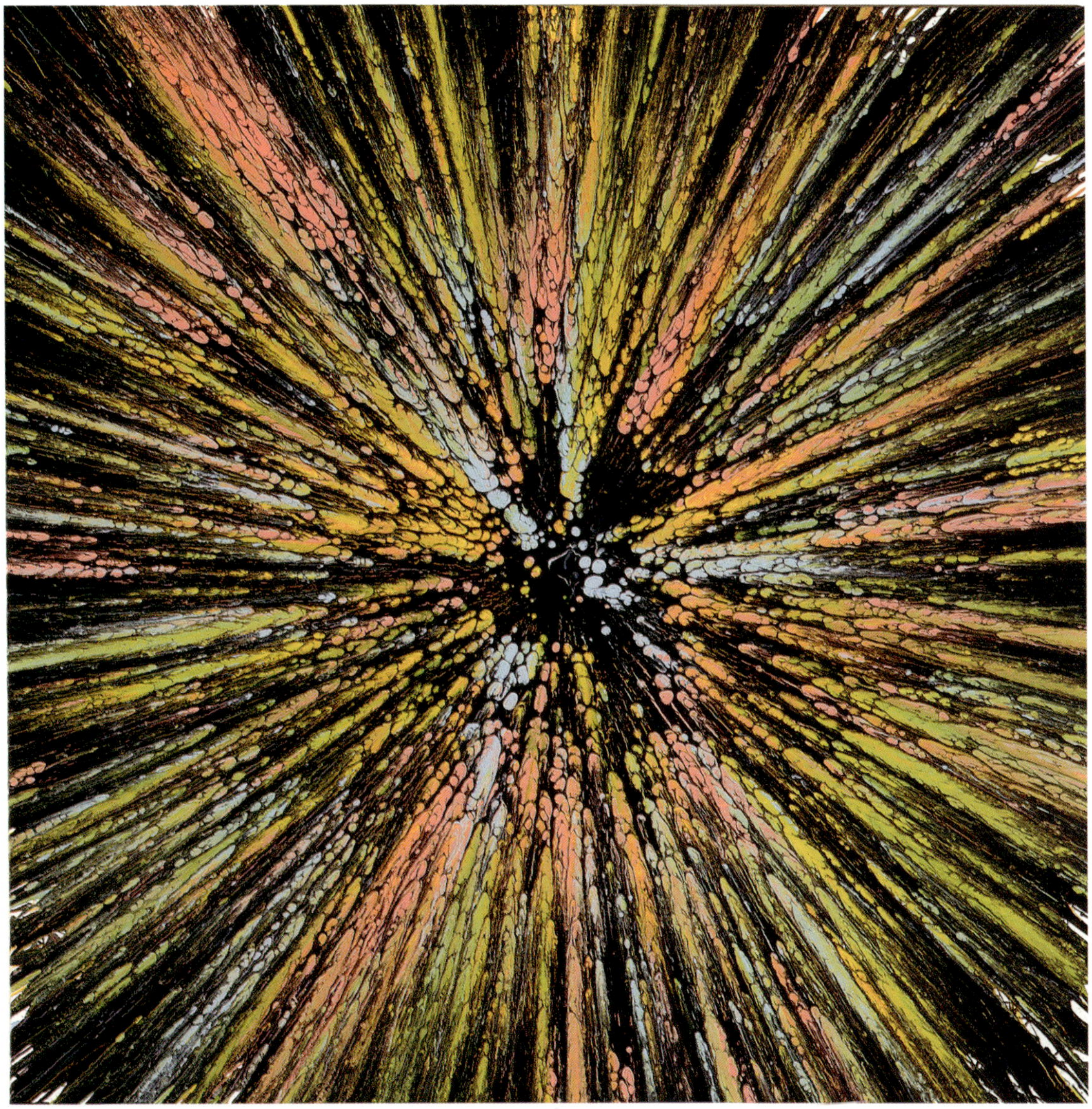

I am Mad, I am Drowning, 1986, latex and oil enamel on canvas, 36 x 36 inches

susie rosmarin

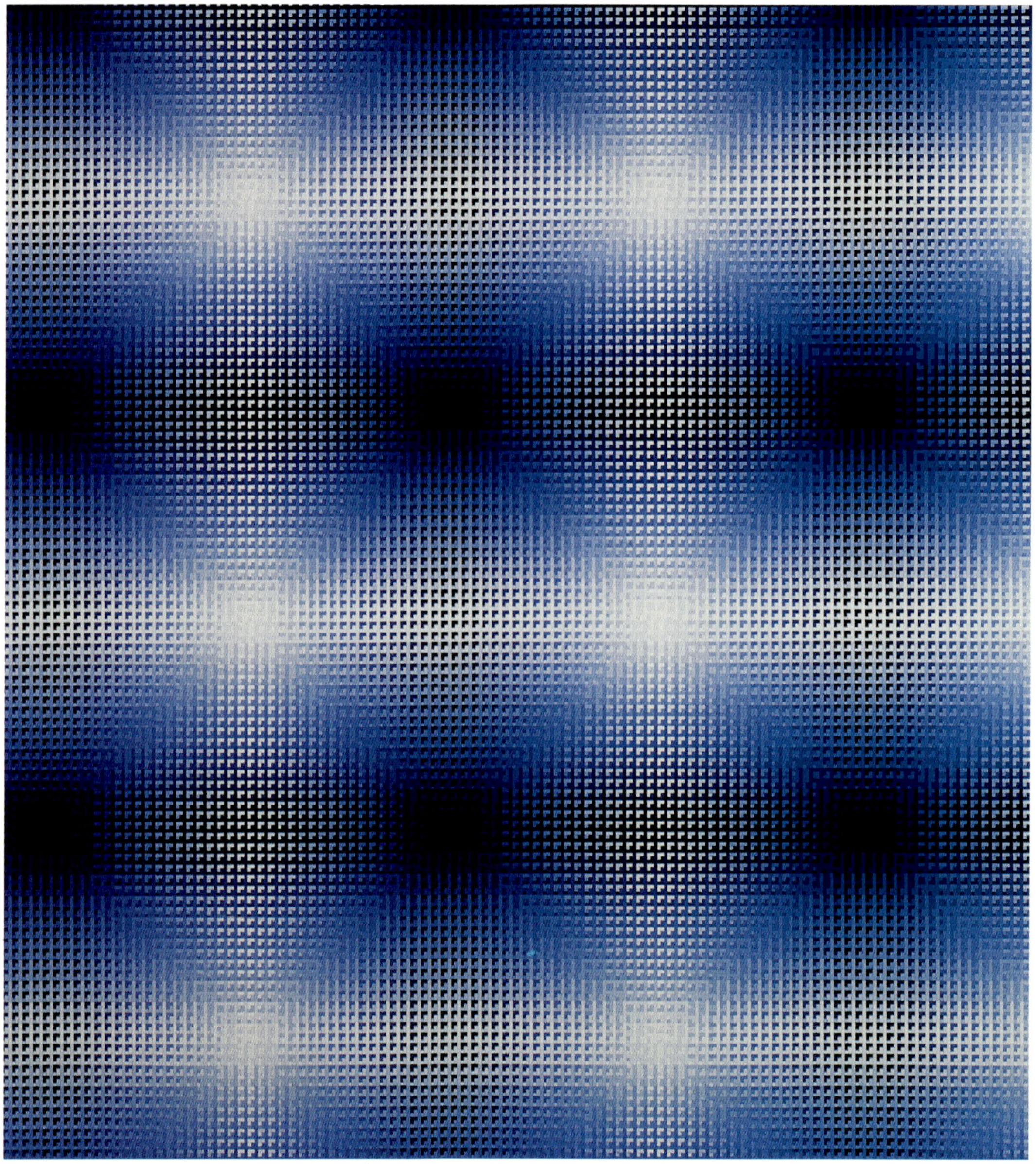

Blue Flash, 1999, acrylic on canvas, 43 x 37 inches
opposite: **Static Study #45 (detail)**, 1998, acrylic on canvas, 84 x 71 inches

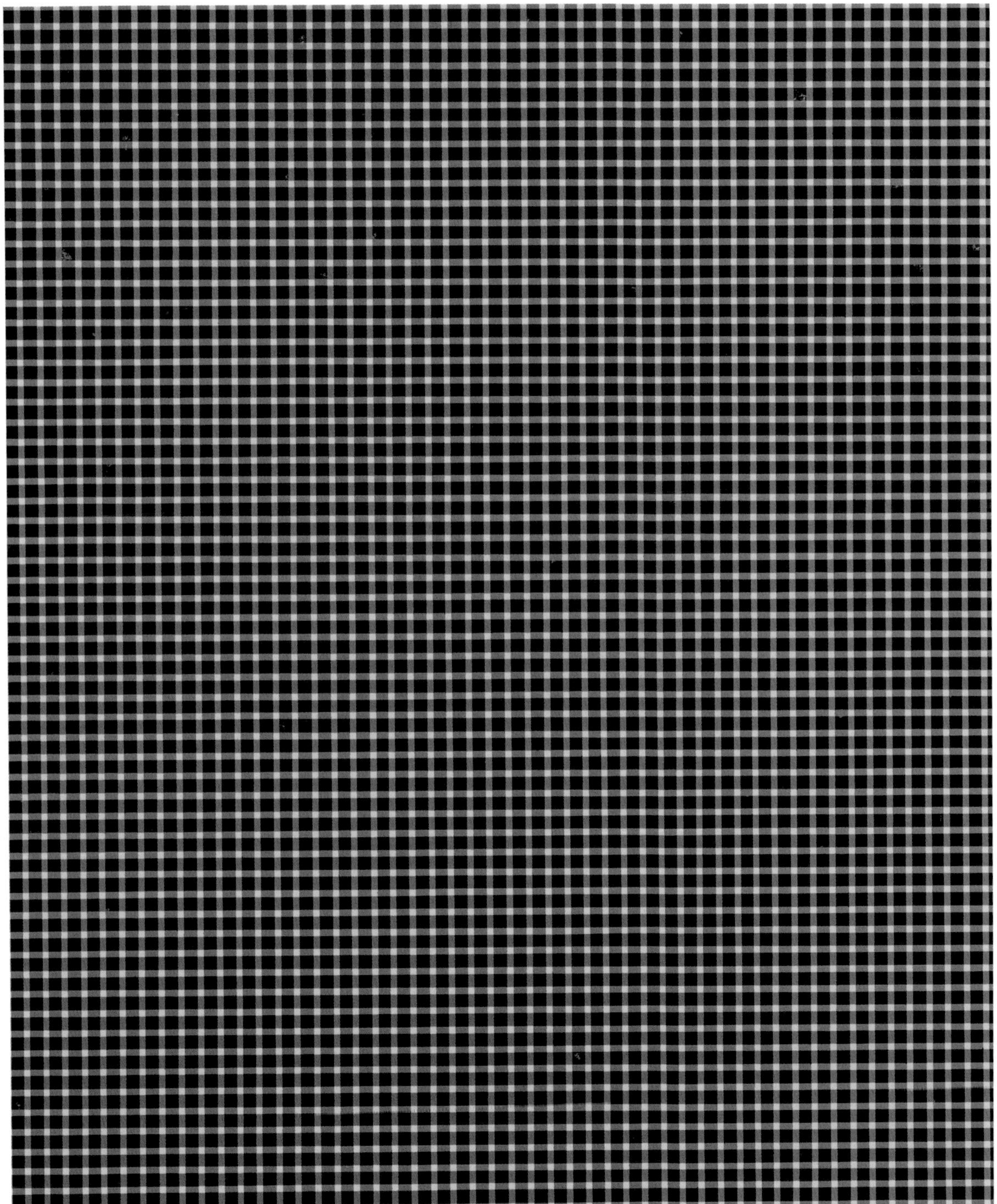

born: 1950, brownsville, texas. lives in brooklyn, new york.

Painting with masking tape is a vaguely erotic activity. Control, release, precision, effusion—it's all there. You mask the naked skin, protecting some areas, exposing others. Ejaculate and peel.[1]

susie rosmarin takes the psychological principle of "periodic structures"—or the repetition of simple geometric patterns—to new heights, embodying in single paintings a virtual anthology of the most alluring effects found in optically-charged abstraction. Generating all sorts of phantom colors (yellows, greens, pinks, purples, blues), fugitive diamond patterns, and flickering after-images, her intricately painted-and-masked gridworks seem also to encompass a shifting spatial matrix of successive screens, with certain horizontal and vertical stripes appearing to hover several inches in front of others—somewhere between the painting's surface and the viewer. Critic Tim Porges has observed that: ". . . Rosmarin's grids push the vibrational, hypnotic potential of the grid to its limit without losing its history as a meditational space. Her paintings are like steroid-enhanced Agnes Martins . . ."[2]

[1]Mark Flood, "Hines and His Circle: Tragic Fading Supergraphic," exhibition catalogue, Art of This Century, Houston, 1998.
[2]Tim Porges, "A Demolition Derby of Art," *The Octopus*, January 15-21, p. 11.

detail: **Static #40**, 1998, acrylic on canvas, 24 x 20 inches
Courtesy the artist, Texas Gallery, Houston, and
Angstrom Gallery, Dallas

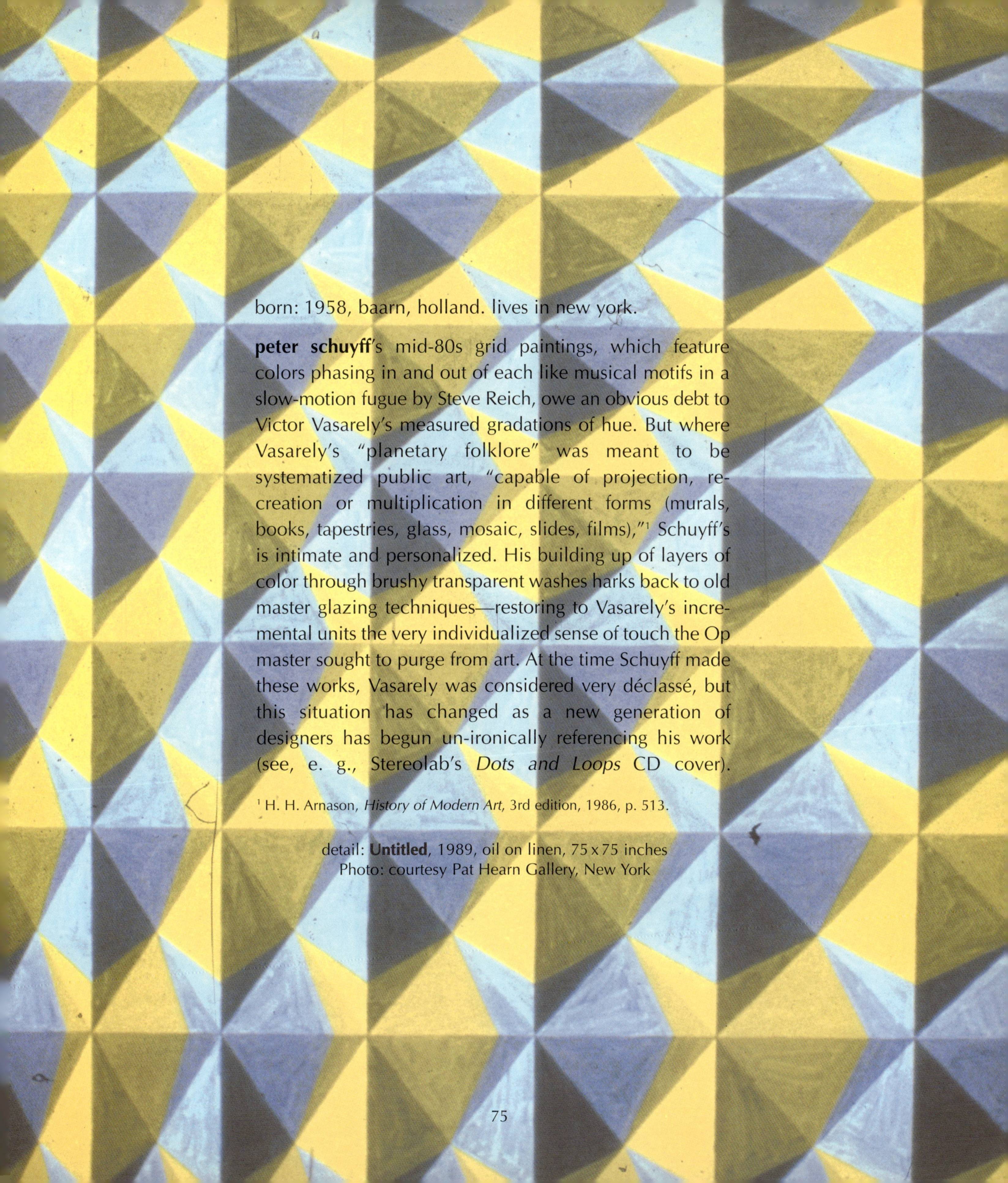

born: 1958, baarn, holland. lives in new york.

peter schuyff's mid-80s grid paintings, which feature colors phasing in and out of each like musical motifs in a slow-motion fugue by Steve Reich, owe an obvious debt to Victor Vasarely's measured gradations of hue. But where Vasarely's "planetary folklore" was meant to be systematized public art, "capable of projection, re-creation or multiplication in different forms (murals, books, tapestries, glass, mosaic, slides, films),"[1] Schuyff's is intimate and personalized. His building up of layers of color through brushy transparent washes harks back to old master glazing techniques—restoring to Vasarely's incremental units the very individualized sense of touch the Op master sought to purge from art. At the time Schuyff made these works, Vasarely was considered very déclassé, but this situation has changed as a new generation of designers has begun un-ironically referencing his work (see, e. g., Stereolab's *Dots and Loops* CD cover).

[1] H. H. Arnason, *History of Modern Art*, 3rd edition, 1986, p. 513.

detail: **Untitled**, 1989, oil on linen, 75 x 75 inches
Photo: courtesy Pat Hearn Gallery, New York

peter schuyff

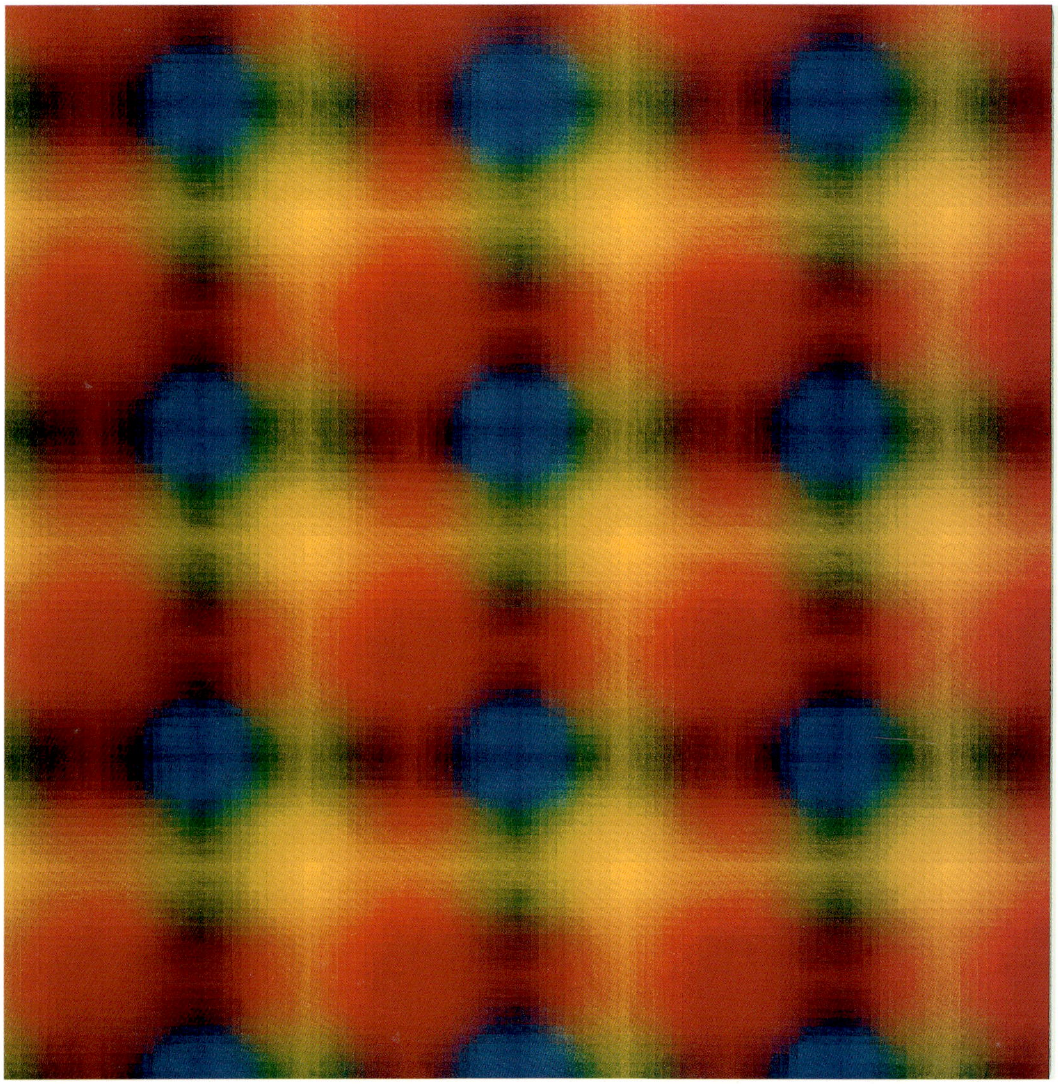

Untitled, 1987, acrylic on linen, 120 x 120 inches
opposite: **Untitled**, 1986, acrylic on linen, 90 x 66 inches

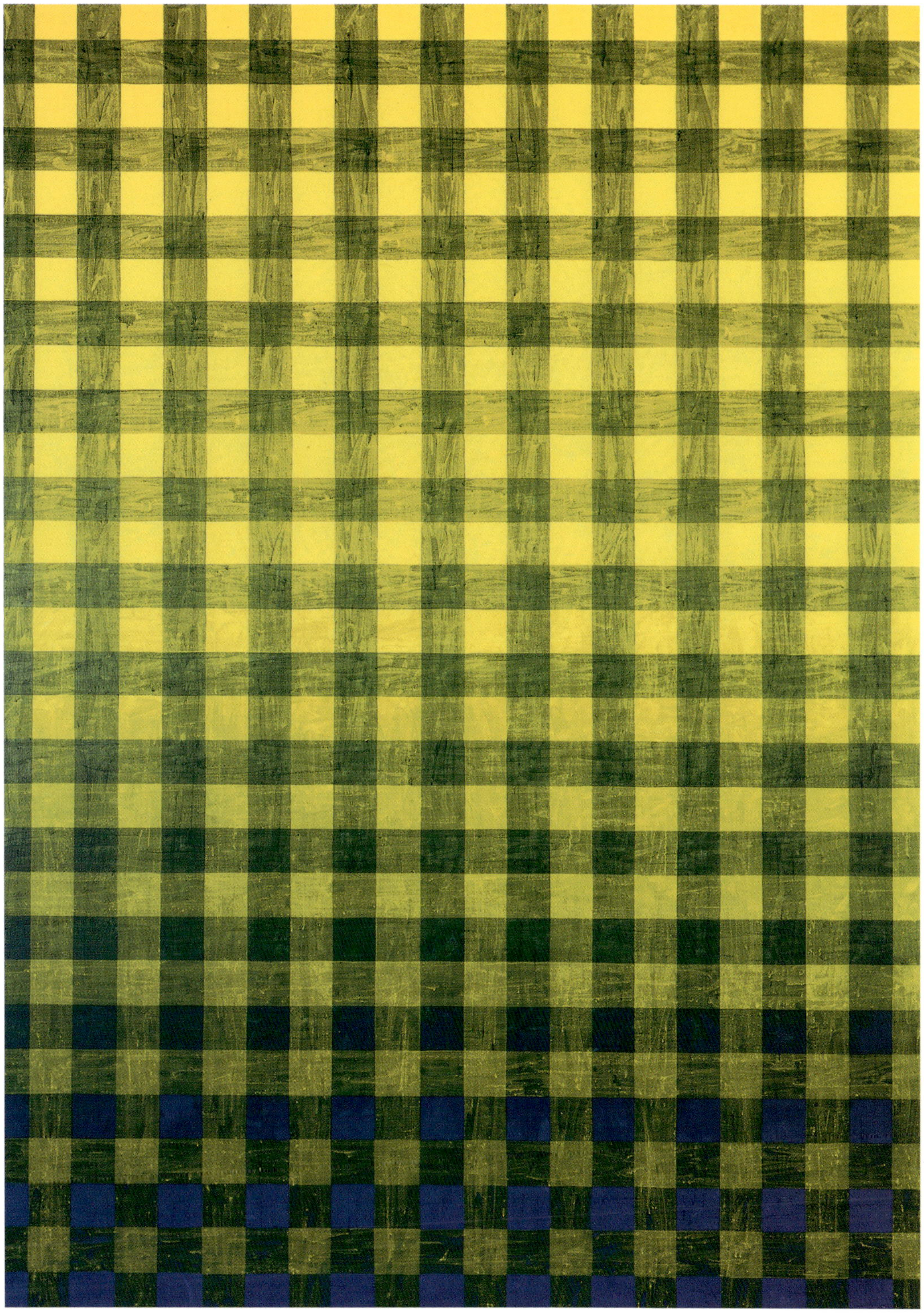

michael scott

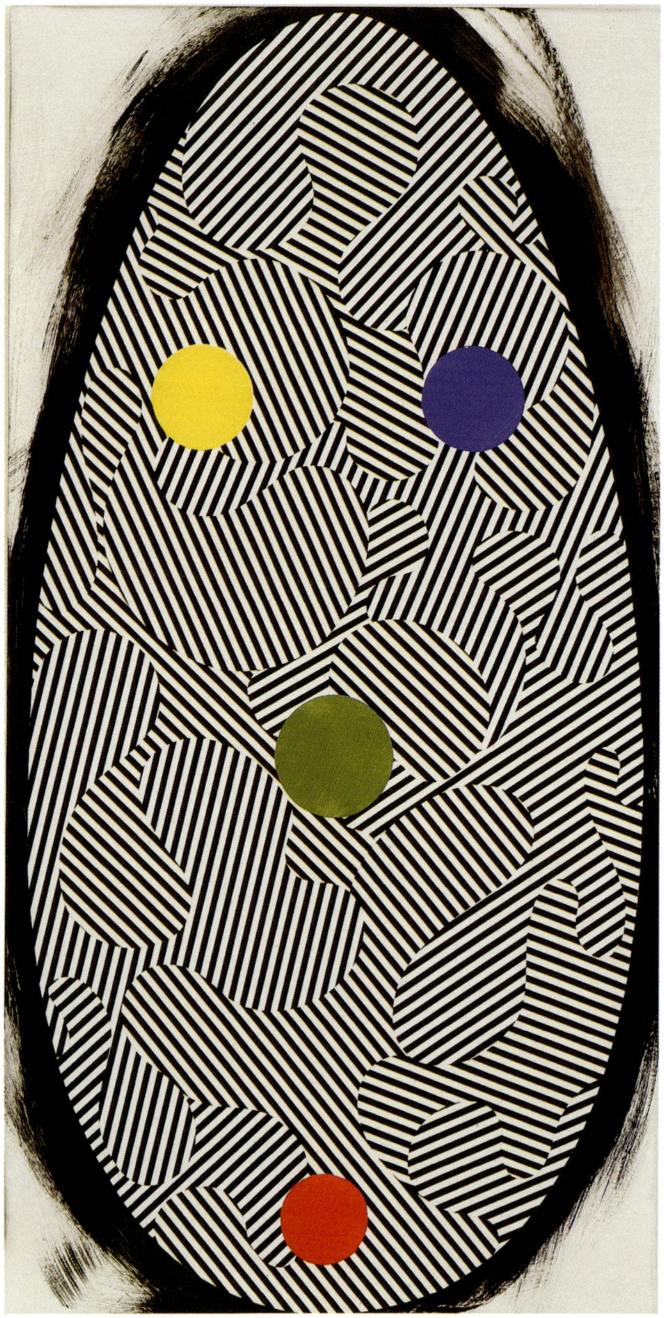

Untitled, 1999, enamel on aluminum, 33 x 17 inches
opposite: **The History of Memory Part 1**, 1993, enamel on aluminum, 78 x 59 inches

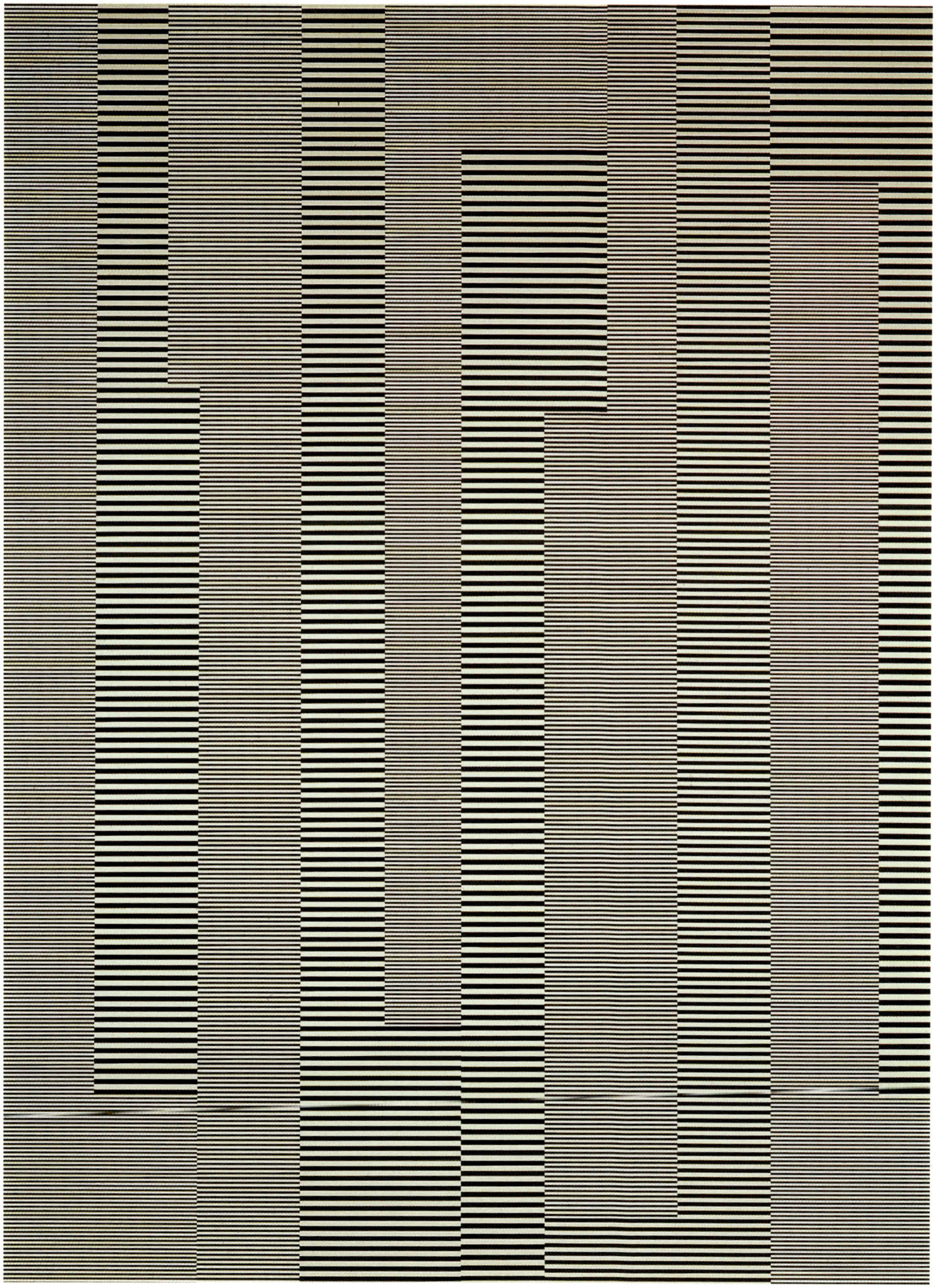

born: 1958, paoli, pennsylvania. lives in long island city.

Certain patterns—stripes receding to a vanishing point, tightly spaced parallel bands—have a disturbing effect on the (human) perceptual system, causing imaginary vibrations. One theory for this is the principle of "redundancy"—that the brain is receiving far more information than it needs when it's perfectly capable of extrapolating a pattern from a small number of visual cues.[1] While Op art in the 60s used this effect to create a kind of upbeat visual jazz, **michael scott**'s unnaturally sharp, dense lines painted on supersmooth aluminum panels take it to near-traumatic extremes, inducing vertigo and hallucinatory sprays of color. Expressing a punkish nihilism at odds with the "swinging 60s," Scott has spoken of his wish to make paintings that are "impossible to look at" or "deny their own viewing;" "I sometimes relate them to Lichtenstein's mirror paintings, where the subject is empty space—a space that exists outside of the painting in which nothing is present."[2] Recent work incorporating cartoon drips and dopey, geometric clown faces adds a hint of perverse humor to the aggressive blankness of these vibrating planes.

[1]R.L. Gregory, *Eye and Brain*, 1976, p. 133.
[2]from an interview with Robert Nickas in *The Void Each Time*, Edizioni Galleria in Arco, Torino, Italy, 1992, p. 18.

detail: **Untitled**, 1999, enamel on aluminum, 30 x 24 inches
Courtesy Sandra Gering Gallery, New York

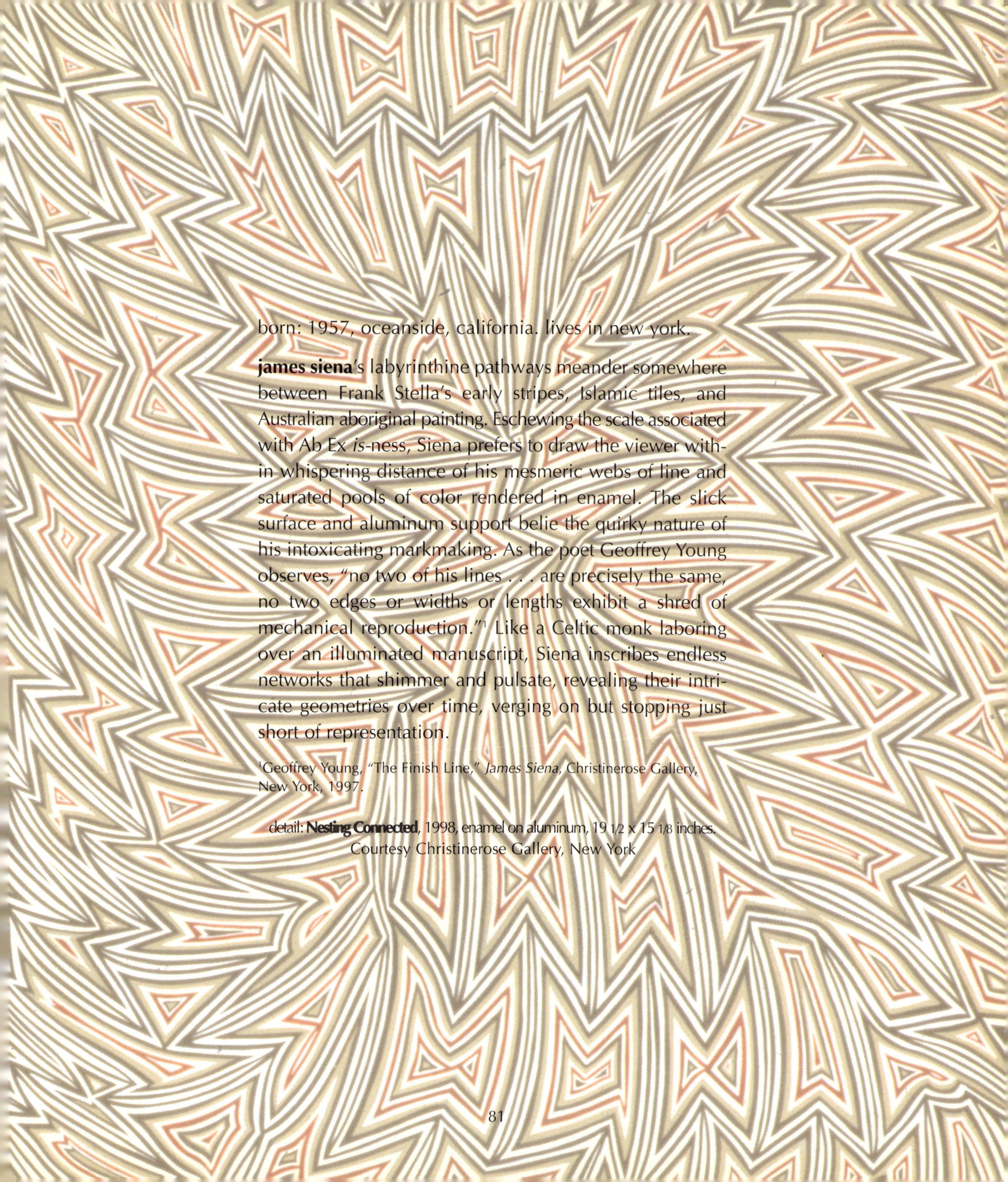

born: 1957, oceanside, california. lives in new york.

james siena's labyrinthine pathways meander somewhere between Frank Stella's early stripes, Islamic tiles, and Australian aboriginal painting. Eschewing the scale associated with Ab Ex *is*-ness, Siena prefers to draw the viewer within whispering distance of his mesmeric webs of line and saturated pools of color rendered in enamel. The slick surface and aluminum support belie the quirky nature of his intoxicating markmaking. As the poet Geoffrey Young observes, "no two of his lines . . . are precisely the same, no two edges or widths or lengths exhibit a shred of mechanical reproduction."[1] Like a Celtic monk laboring over an illuminated manuscript, Siena inscribes endless networks that shimmer and pulsate, revealing their intricate geometries over time, verging on but stopping just short of representation.

[1]Geoffrey Young, "The Finish Line," *James Siena*, Christinerose Gallery, New York, 1997.

detail: **Nesting Connected**, 1998, enamel on aluminum, 19 1/2 x 15 1/8 inches.
Courtesy Christinerose Gallery, New York

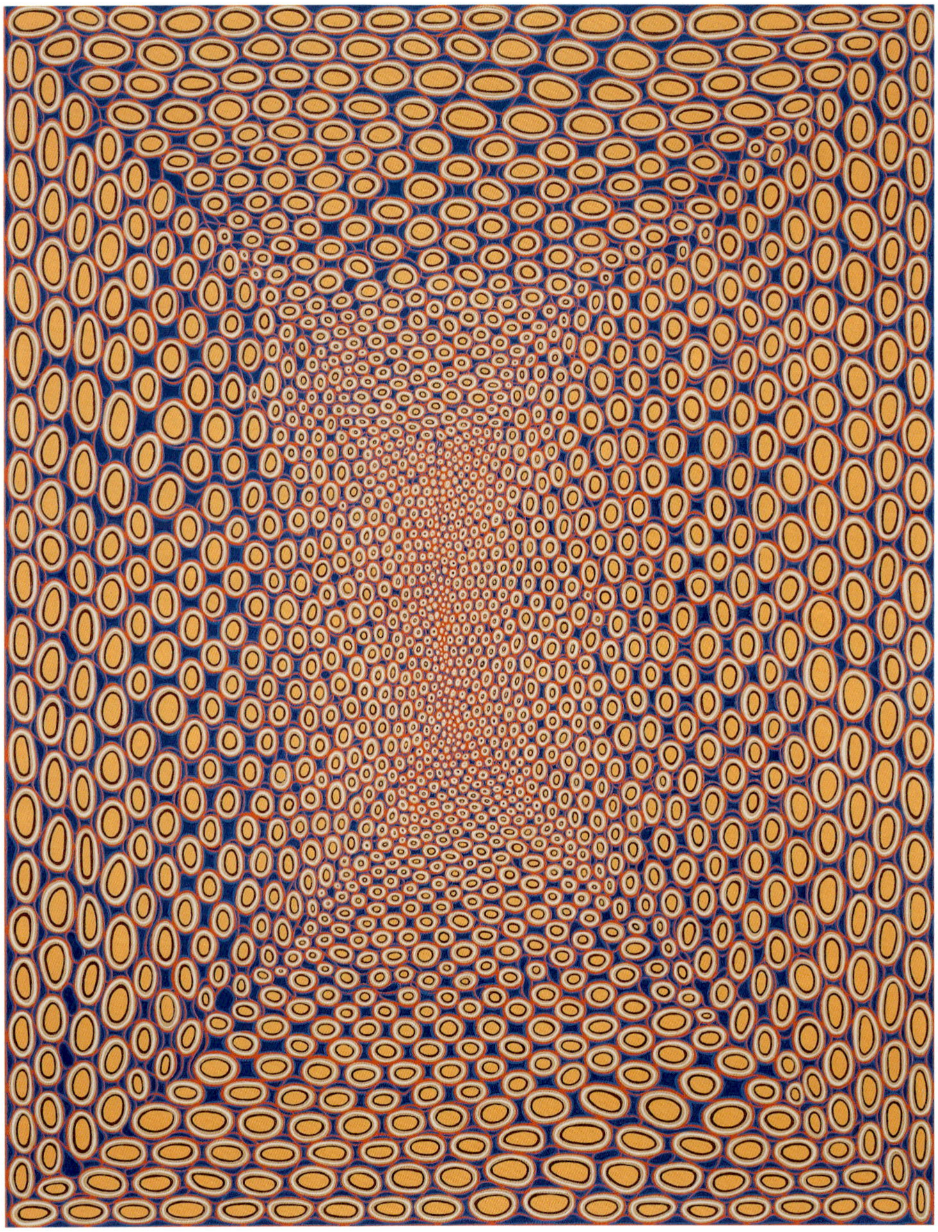

Battery, 1997, enamel on aluminum, 29 x 22 3/4 inches

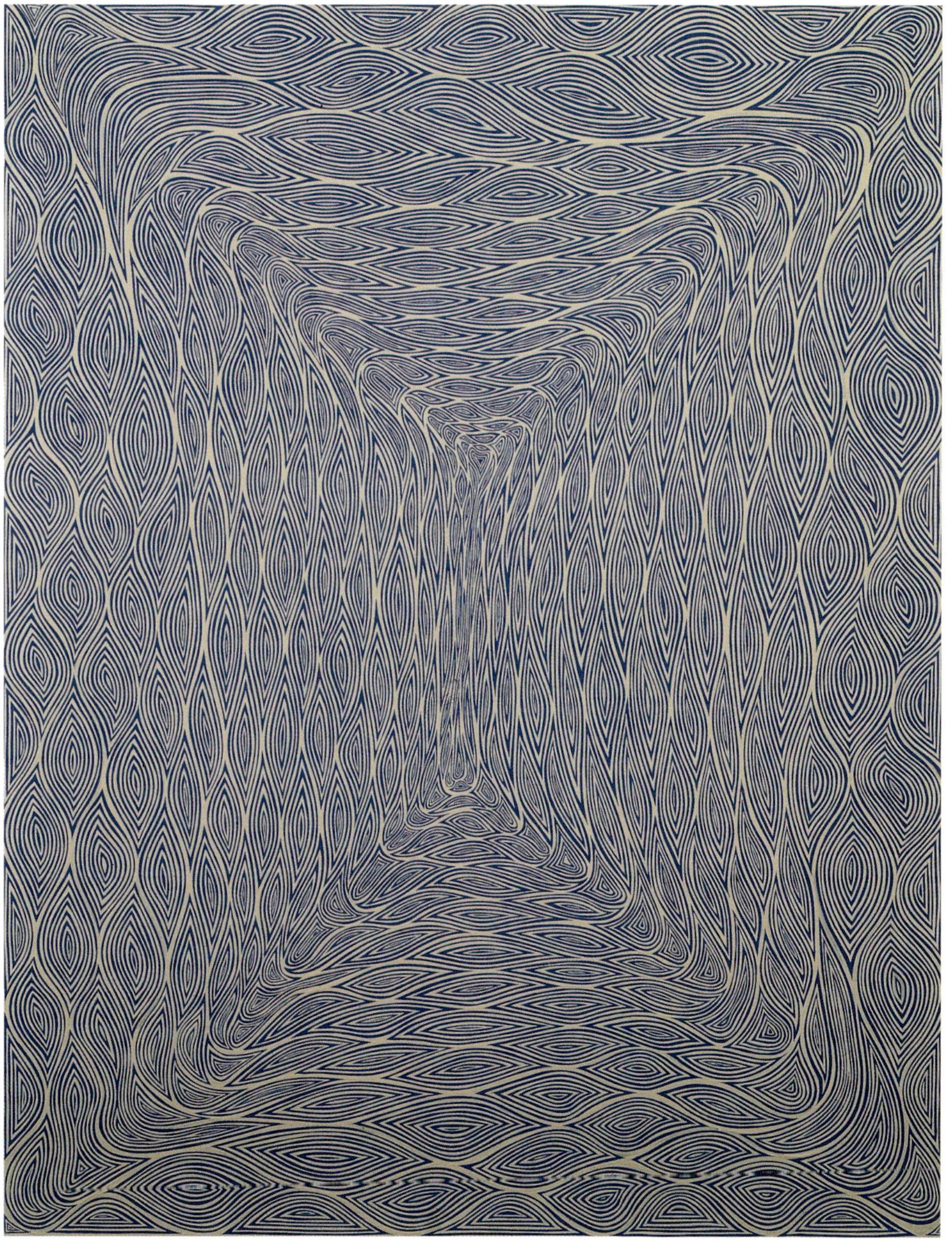

Twirly Three, 1995, enamel on aluminum, 29 x 22 3/4 inches

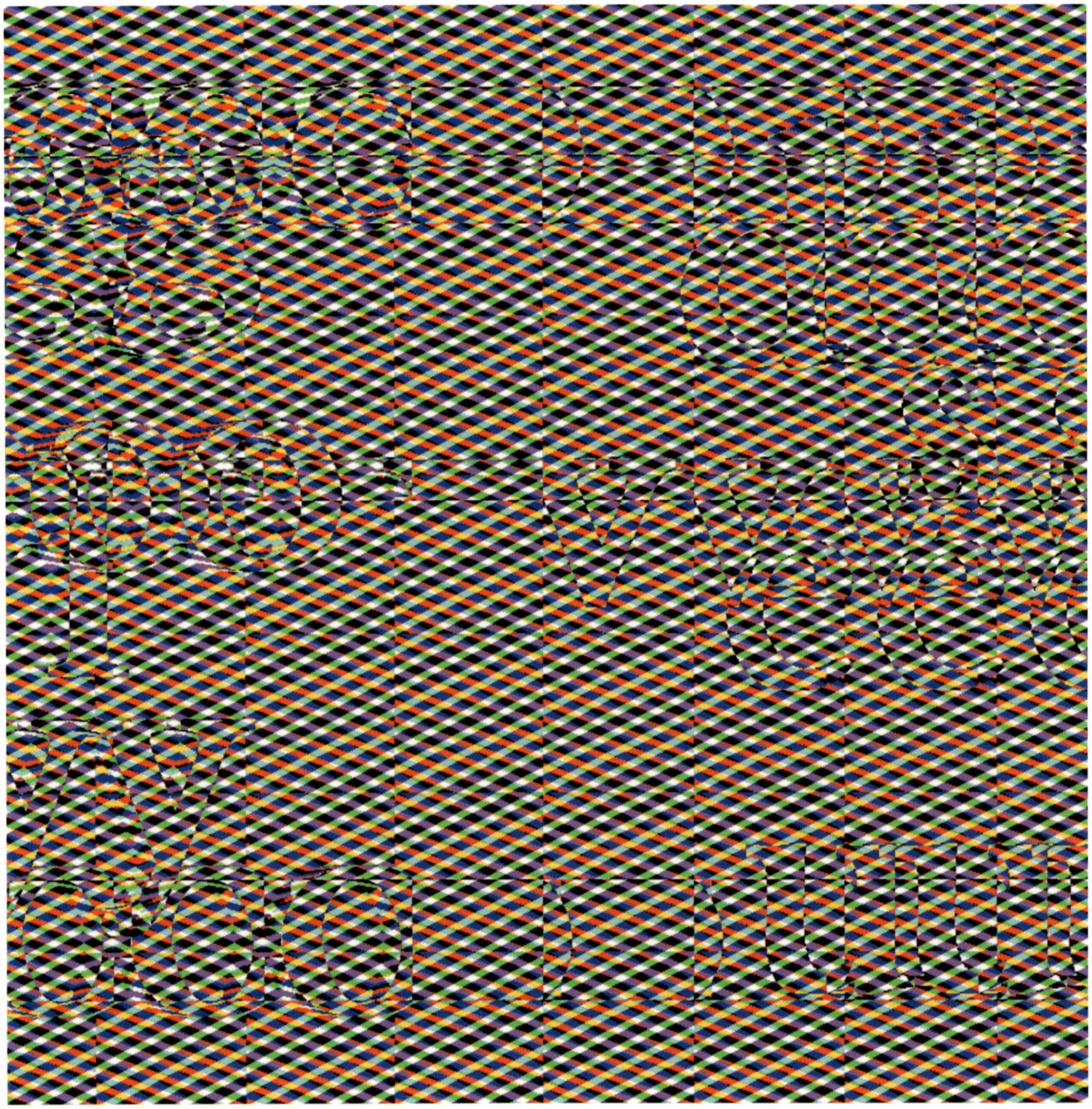

God is in the Details, 1998, digital ink jet print on paper, variable dimensions

david szafranski

Bra Sale, 1998, digital ink jet print on paper, variable dimensions

born: 1959 in the u.s. lives in paris.

david szafranski's medium is the "random dot stereogram," popularly known as the "Magic Eye" illusion, which initially resembles a grainy field but slowly reveals optically encoded words as the viewer's eyes become acclimated to the pattern (not everyone can see them). Printed out on large-scale digital plotters and hung on the wall at eye level, these seductive, two- and three-color fields look like abstract art, but once viewers learn they contain hidden messages, the artist says, "they'll look at them much longer than they would abstractions." One seeking profound meaning in these voids may be disappointed, however, since the messages are generally pretty stupid. After gazing patiently at **Grande Crème de la Cuisse**, 1995, for example, the viewer is rewarded with a glimpse of the words "thigh cream," while the would-be voyeur (or shopper) drawn to **Bra Sale**, 1998, is told to "stop staring."

detail: **I'm PG**, 1998, digital ink jet print on paper, variable dimensions. Courtesy the artist

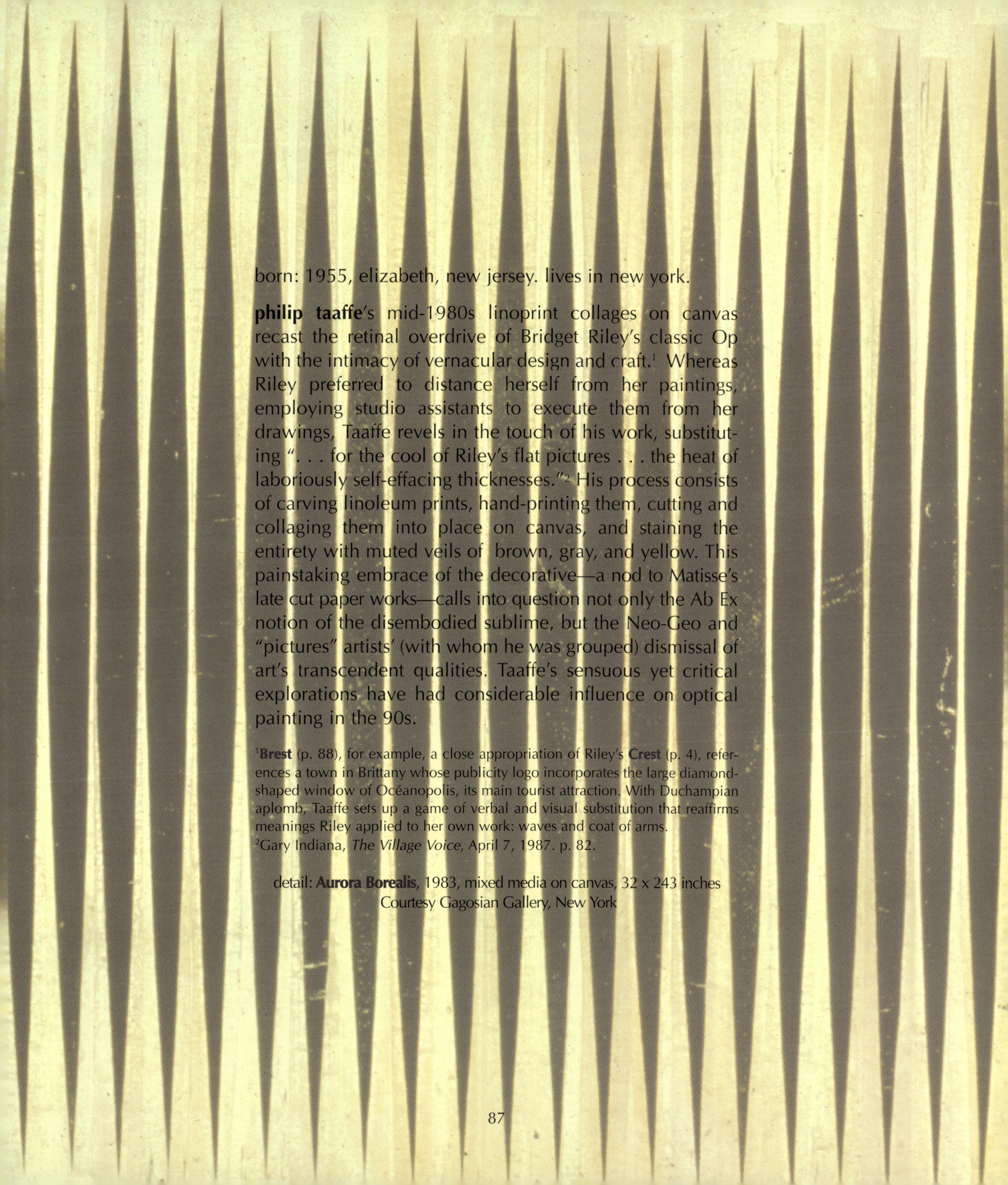

born: 1955, elizabeth, new jersey. lives in new york.

philip taaffe's mid-1980s linoprint collages on canvas recast the retinal overdrive of Bridget Riley's classic Op with the intimacy of vernacular design and craft.[1] Whereas Riley preferred to distance herself from her paintings, employing studio assistants to execute them from her drawings, Taaffe revels in the touch of his work, substituting ". . . for the cool of Riley's flat pictures . . . the heat of laboriously self-effacing thicknesses."[2] His process consists of carving linoleum prints, hand-printing them, cutting and collaging them into place on canvas, and staining the entirety with muted veils of brown, gray, and yellow. This painstaking embrace of the decorative—a nod to Matisse's late cut paper works—calls into question not only the Ab Ex notion of the disembodied sublime, but the Neo-Geo and "pictures" artists' (with whom he was grouped) dismissal of art's transcendent qualities. Taaffe's sensuous yet critical explorations have had considerable influence on optical painting in the 90s.

[1]**Brest** (p. 88), for example, a close appropriation of Riley's **Crest** (p. 4), references a town in Brittany whose publicity logo incorporates the large diamond-shaped window of Océanopolis, its main tourist attraction. With Duchampian aplomb, Taaffe sets up a game of verbal and visual substitution that reaffirms meanings Riley applied to her own work: waves and coat of arms.
[2]Gary Indiana, *The Village Voice*, April 7, 1987. p. 82.

detail: **Aurora Borealis**, 1983, mixed media on canvas, 32 x 243 inches
Courtesy Gagosian Gallery, New York

philip taaffe

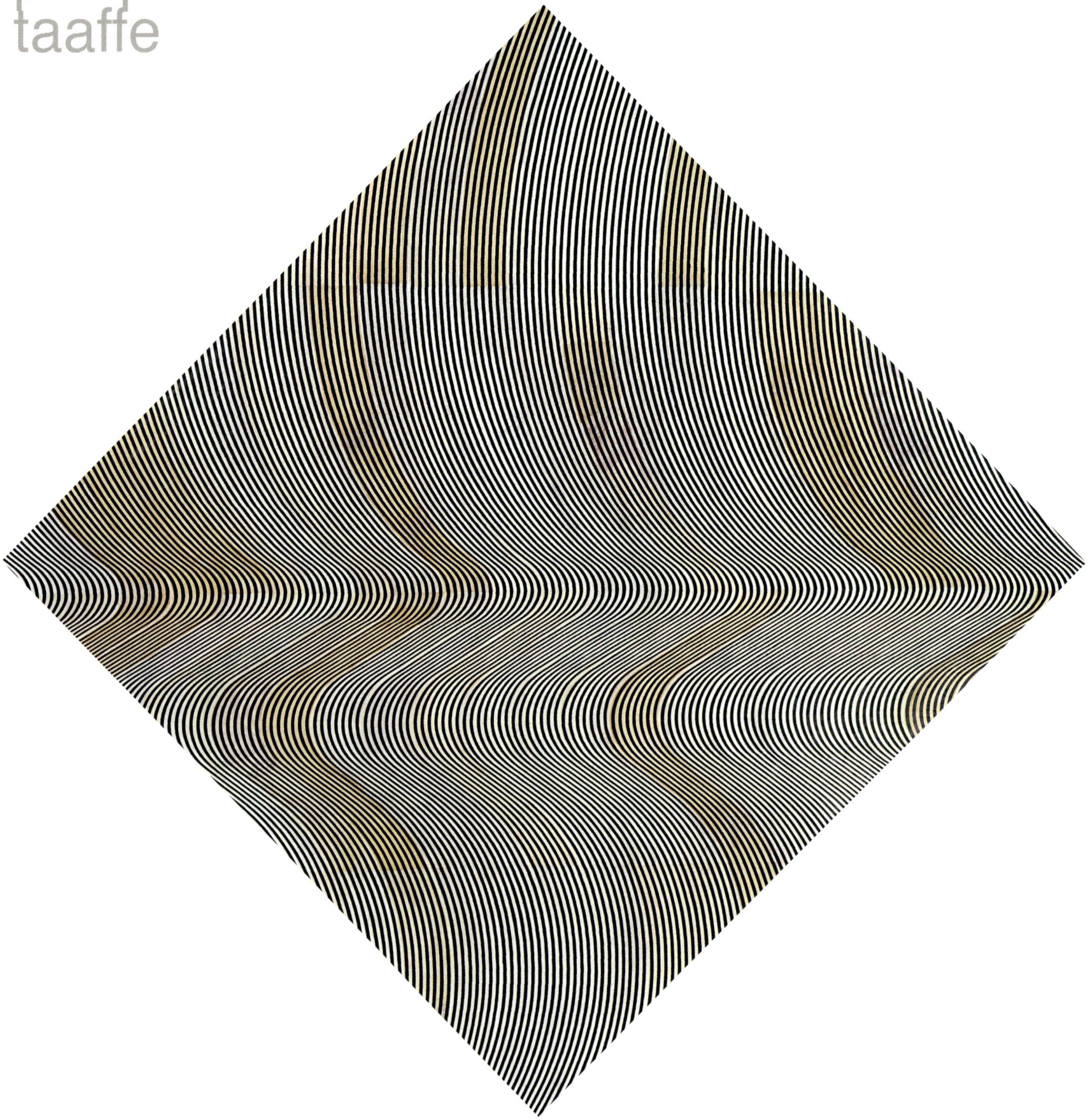

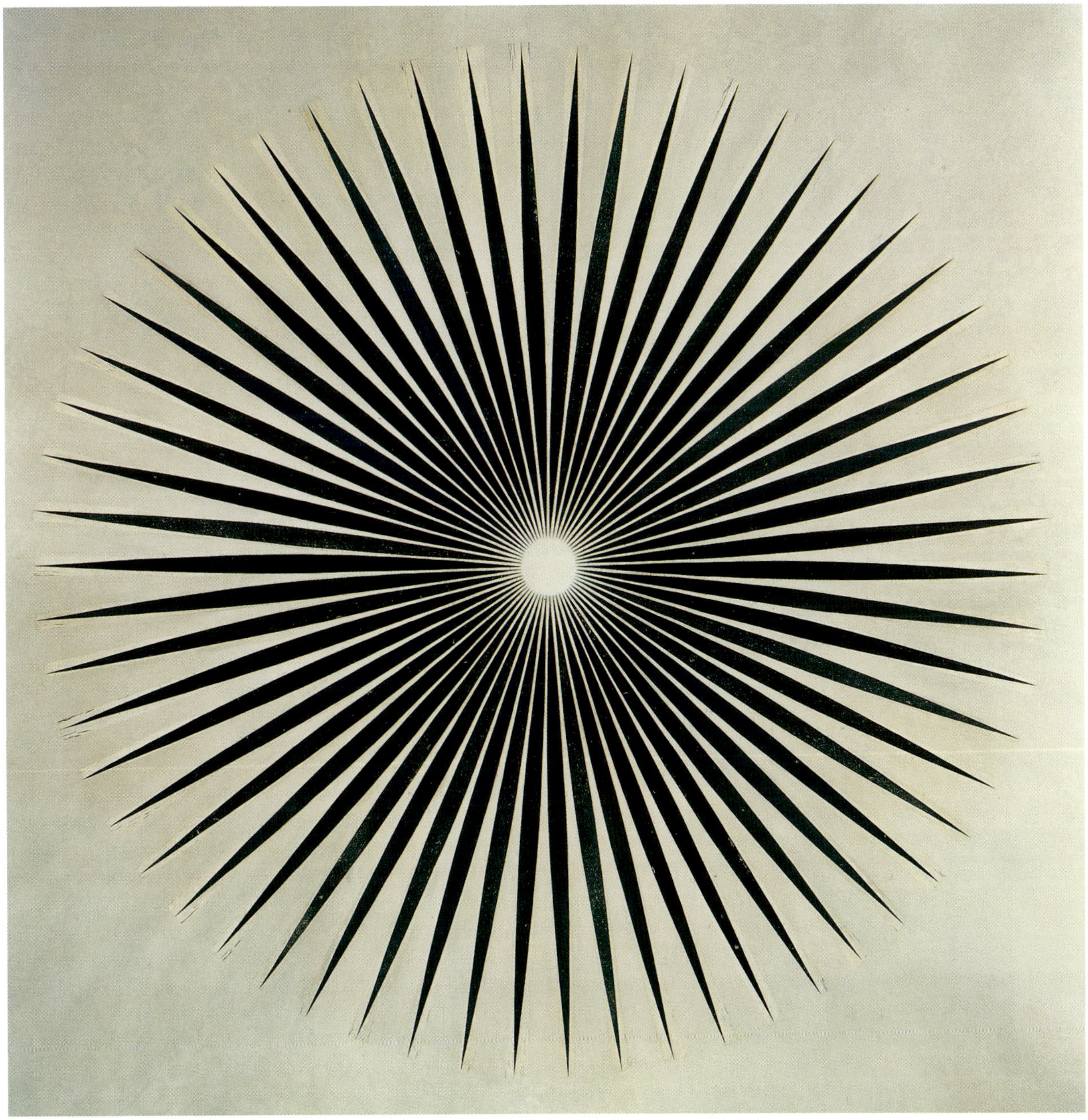

Big Iris, 1985, linoprint collage and acrylic on canvas, 63 x 63 inches
opposite: **Brest**, 1985, linoprint collage and acrylic on canvas, 110 3/4 x 110 3/4 inches

fred tomaselli

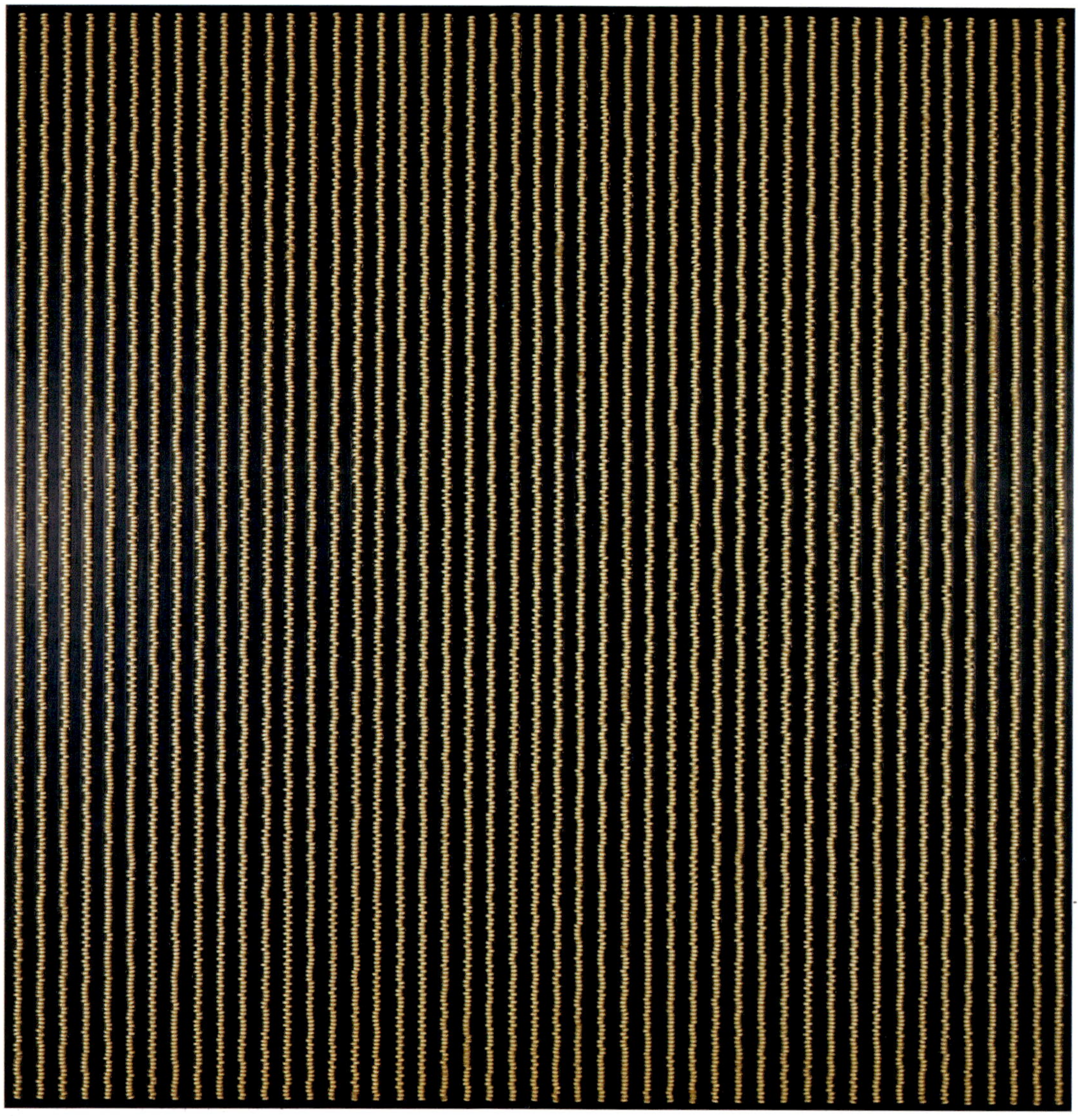

Thirteen Thousand, 1992, aspirin, acrylic, and resin on wood, 48 x 47 inches
opposite: **Bird Blast**, 1997, leaves, pills, collage, synthetic polymer paint and resin on wood, 60 x 60 inches

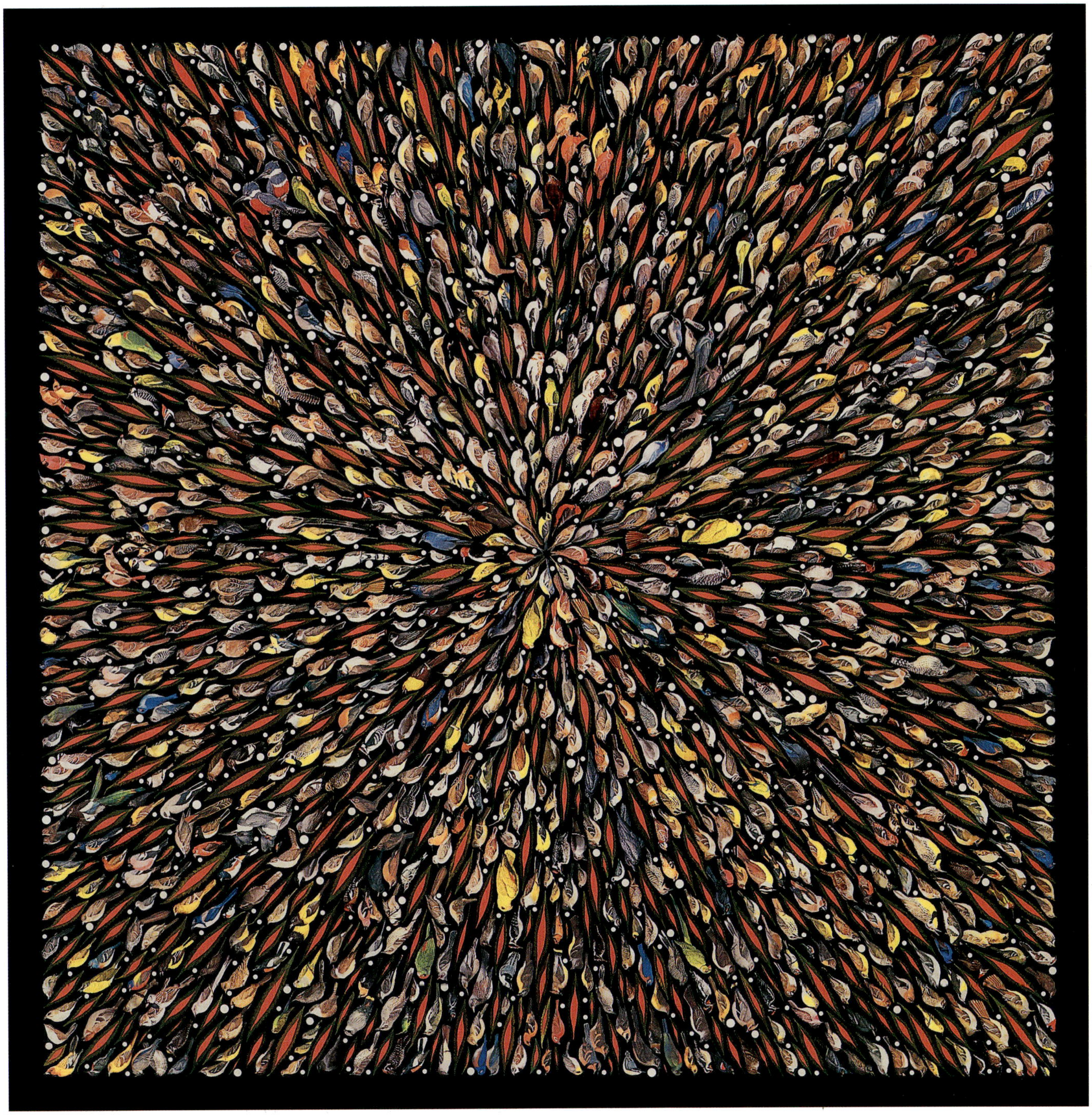

born: 1956, santa monica, california. lives in brooklyn, new york.

Embedded in clear resin like insects in amber, **fred tomaselli**'s intricately arranged pills and marijuana leaves combine with painted or printed elements, alluding to art's transportive potential. The artist is unabashedly vocal about his intention to take the viewer to another place. First exhibiting installation art in the late '80s—spotlit styrofoam cups dancing wavelike on floor tarpaulins, propelled by electric fans; planetariumlike boxes you could stick your head into for a private light show—he then made black and white constellation drawings charting friends' legal and illegal drug histories. Since 1991, however, he has produced thick, wall-mounted paintings with intricate arrangements of tablets, capsules, nicotine patches, pot leaves, and other paraphernalia. **Thirteen Thousand** consists of thousands of aspirin tablets arranged in vertical columns; the key to its visual punch is the irregular lineup of pills, bringing to mind misaligned vertebrae, beads on an abacus, or a digital sequence bearing coded information. The resin, with all its vagaries of bubbling, serves to blur the columns, and actually dissolves the tablets, which are frozen forever in a solid but dissipated state.

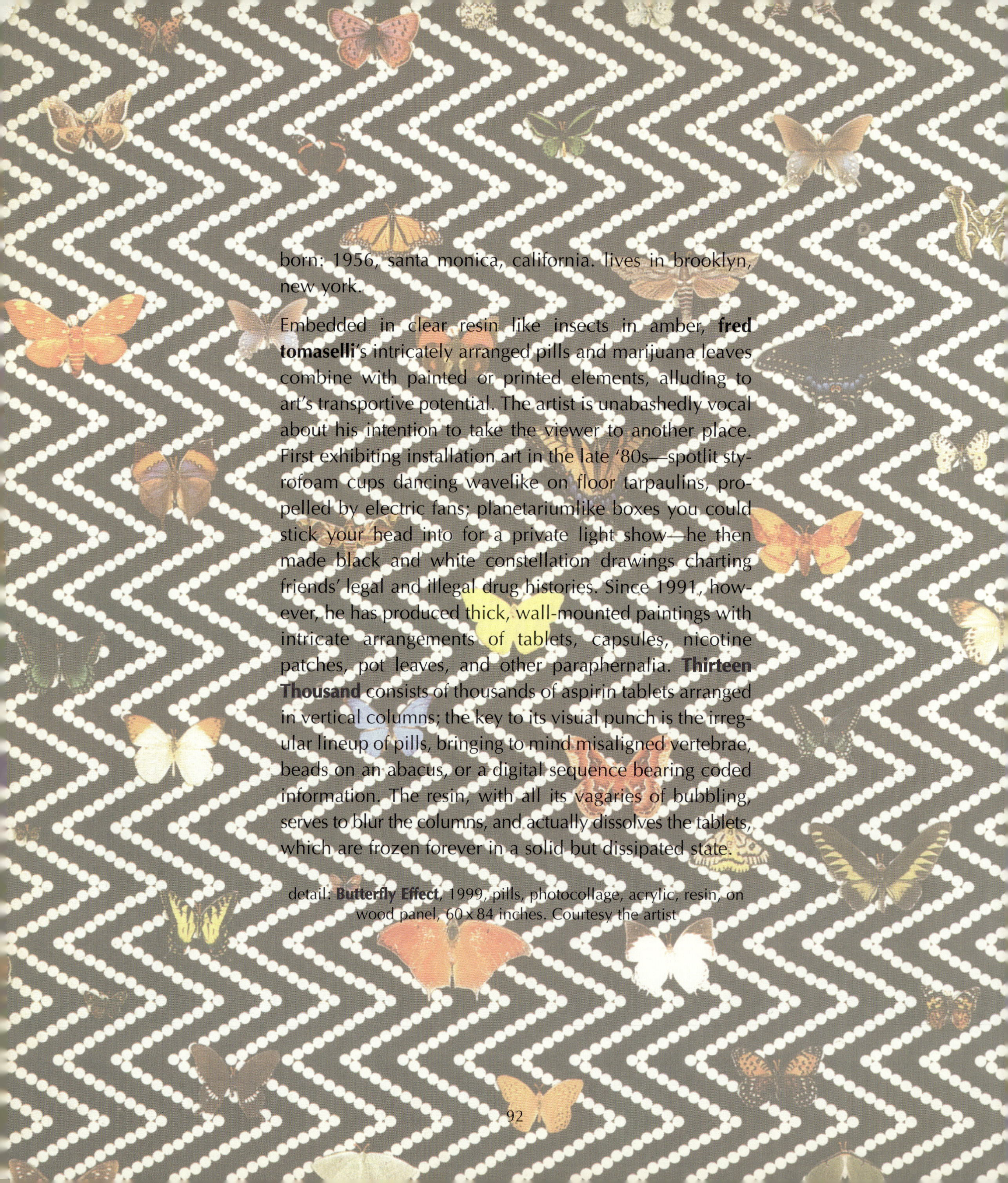

detail: **Butterfly Effect**, 1999, pills, photocollage, acrylic, resin, on wood panel, 60 x 84 inches. Courtesy the artist

born: 1968, singapore. lives in las vegas.

yek comes out of the tangerine sherbety sunset school of Ed Ruscha, substituting for the elder artist's printed aphorisms a thin pinstripe ending with a flourish of mock-Arabic calligraphy. These concave paintings of molded wood reference many aspects of popular art and design, from Von Dutch car striping to tanning mirrors to 60s chair design. Perhaps poking fun at the worship we ascribe to Abstract Expressionist-era paintings ("Did you feel it?"), these chunks of pure atmosphere with skywritten zips passing through the picture plane entrance us with their blatant sensuosity and playfulness—putting Roth (as in Ed "Big Daddy") into Rothko. Sometimes illuminated by black lights to intensify their Day-Glo color schemes, these curving planes become sleek, aeronautically designed objects of contemplation for the modern age.

detail: **Seriously, Nervously, Jealously**, 1998, acrylic and latex on wood, 42 x 42 x 7 inches. Courtesy Post Gallery, Los Angeles

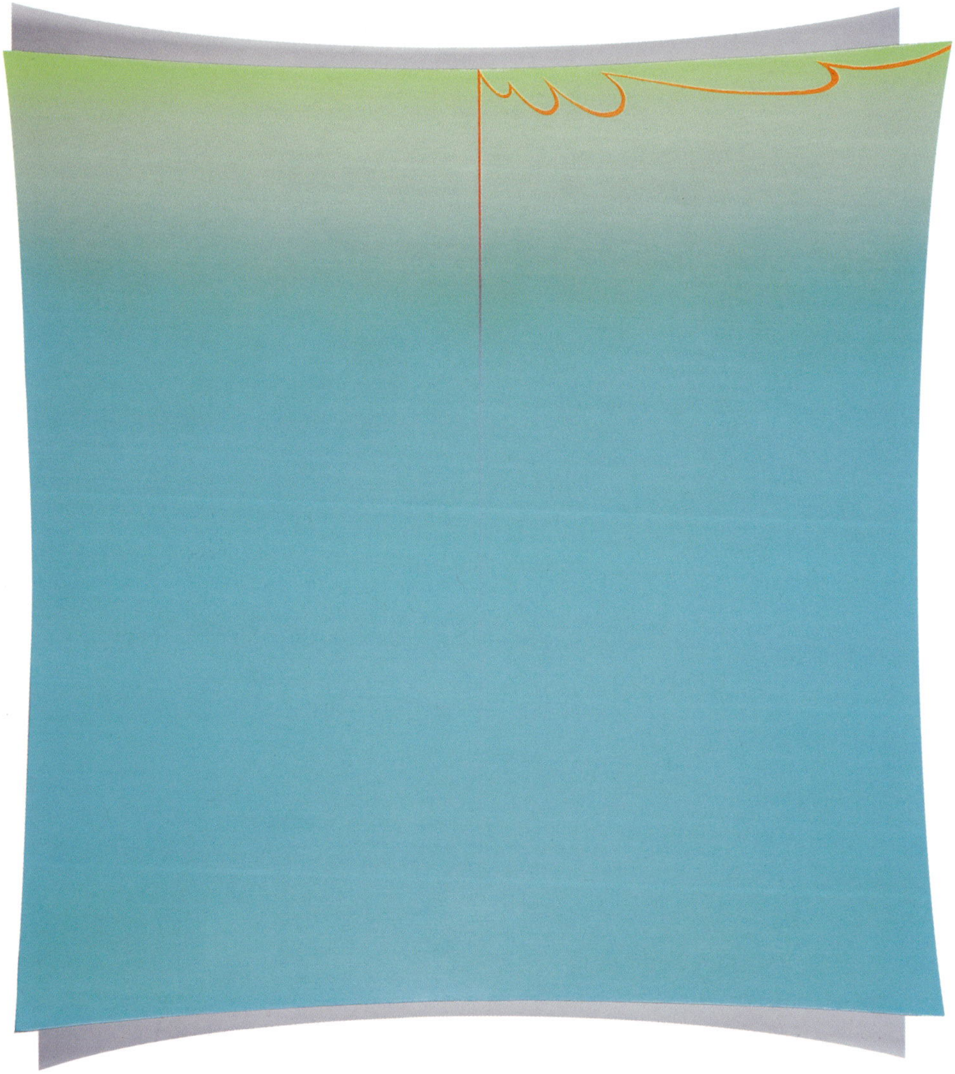

Freefalling Farewell, 1999, acrylic and latex on wood, 30 x 30 x 3 inches

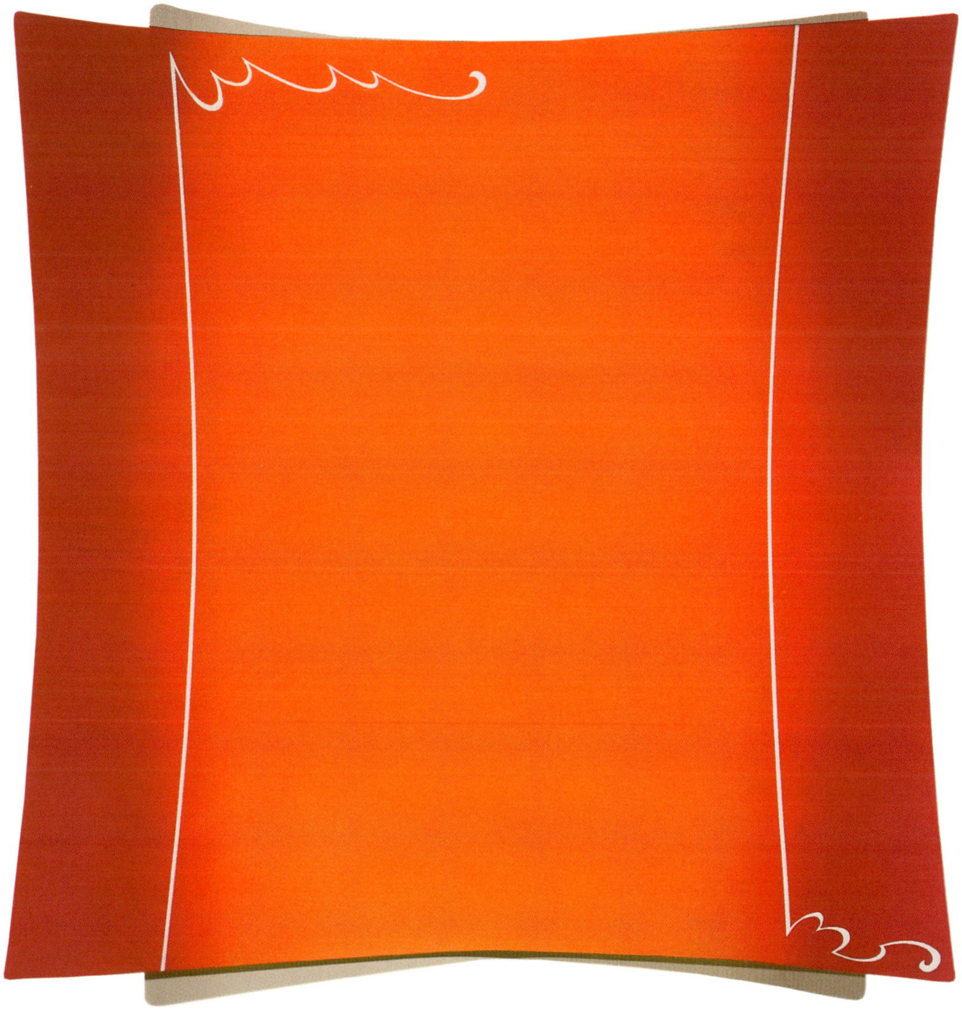

Madness Comes Quickly, 1998, acrylic and latex on wood, 48 x 48 x 7 inches

afterword: some thoughts on "post-hypnotic"

As a title for a show of latter-day optical art, "post-hypnotic" hits the bull's eye on several counts. Obviously it's a sly double entendre, referencing the subliminal messages long suspected to lurk within psychedelic-type art, while at the same time mocking the art world's mania for historical labels. The pun, in turn, puts ironic quotation marks around the exhibit, allowing the artists to participate in a "movement" and at the same time distance themselves from those much-maligned (oversimplified, hegemonic, market-driven) groupings.

As an art-historical neologism, "post-hypnotic" seems absurd on its face. Was an art ever classified solely as "hypnotic"? Can something be over that never actually began? The classic Op art of Bridget Riley and Victor Vasarely—wiggly stripes and kinetic colors reveled in for their own mesmerizing sakes—supposedly ended decades ago. If there has been a sudden spurt of interest in "optical phenomena"—and the work in this show certainly indicates that there has—then why refer to it in the past tense?

Perhaps what's over is not "the hypnotic" but unquestioning belief in the hypnotic. In Op's heyday in the early 60s, audiences accepted the premise (in the film *The Manchurian Candidate*) that an entire patrol of soldiers could be brainwashed—and one of them conditioned to be a remorseless assassin—in a mere three-day time span, whereas now the process would be expected to take . . . oh, at least a month. During that credulous era, science

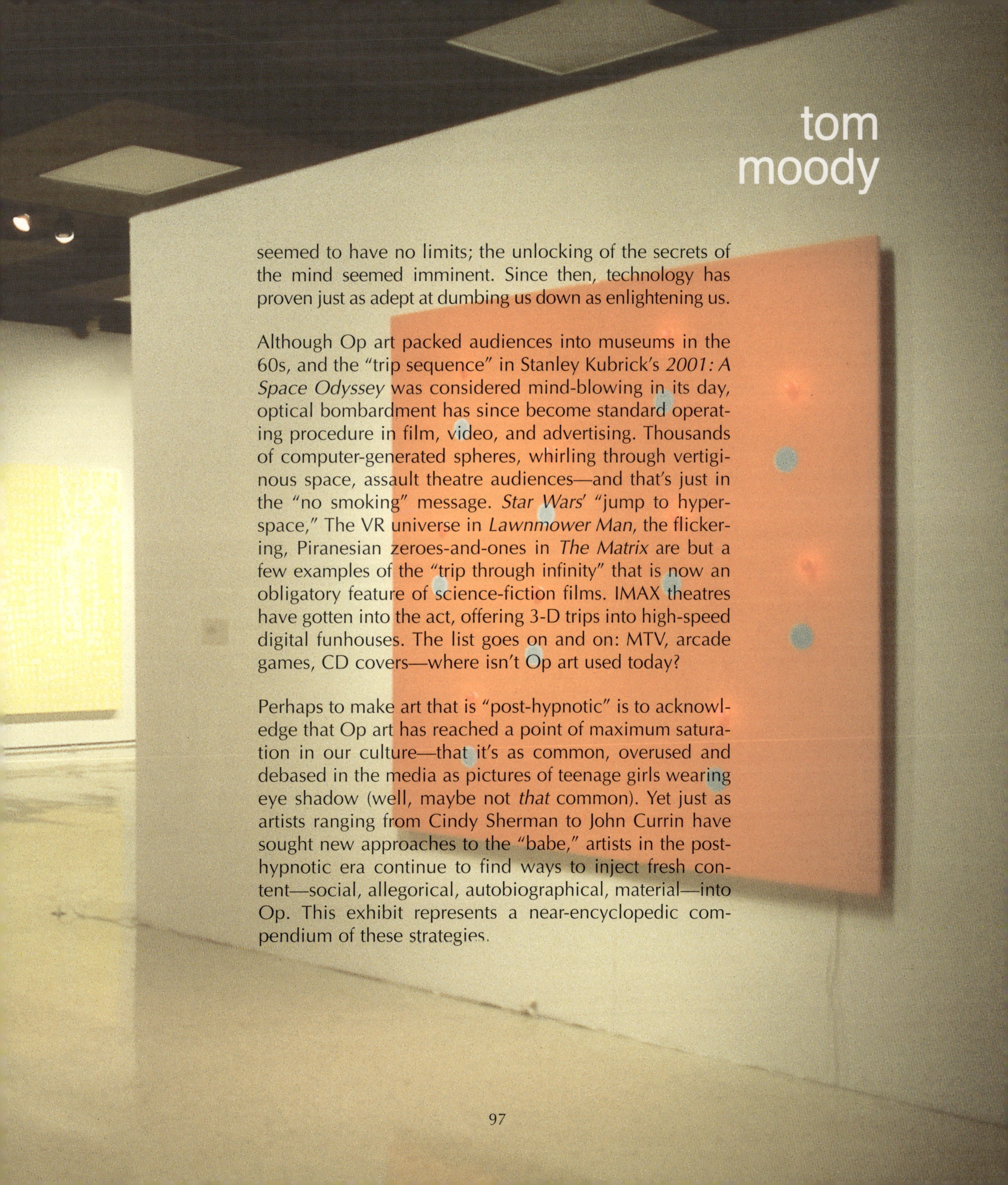

tom moody

seemed to have no limits; the unlocking of the secrets of the mind seemed imminent. Since then, technology has proven just as adept at dumbing us down as enlightening us.

Although Op art packed audiences into museums in the 60s, and the "trip sequence" in Stanley Kubrick's *2001: A Space Odyssey* was considered mind-blowing in its day, optical bombardment has since become standard operating procedure in film, video, and advertising. Thousands of computer-generated spheres, whirling through vertiginous space, assault theatre audiences—and that's just in the "no smoking" message. *Star Wars*' "jump to hyperspace," The VR universe in *Lawnmower Man*, the flickering, Piranesian zeroes-and-ones in *The Matrix* are but a few examples of the "trip through infinity" that is now an obligatory feature of science-fiction films. IMAX theatres have gotten into the act, offering 3-D trips into high-speed digital funhouses. The list goes on and on: MTV, arcade games, CD covers—where isn't Op art used today?

Perhaps to make art that is "post-hypnotic" is to acknowledge that Op art has reached a point of maximum saturation in our culture—that it's as common, overused and debased in the media as pictures of teenage girls wearing eye shadow (well, maybe not *that* common). Yet just as artists ranging from Cindy Sherman to John Currin have sought new approaches to the "babe," artists in the post-hypnotic era continue to find ways to inject fresh content—social, allegorical, autobiographical, material—into Op. This exhibit represents a near-encyclopedic compendium of these strategies.

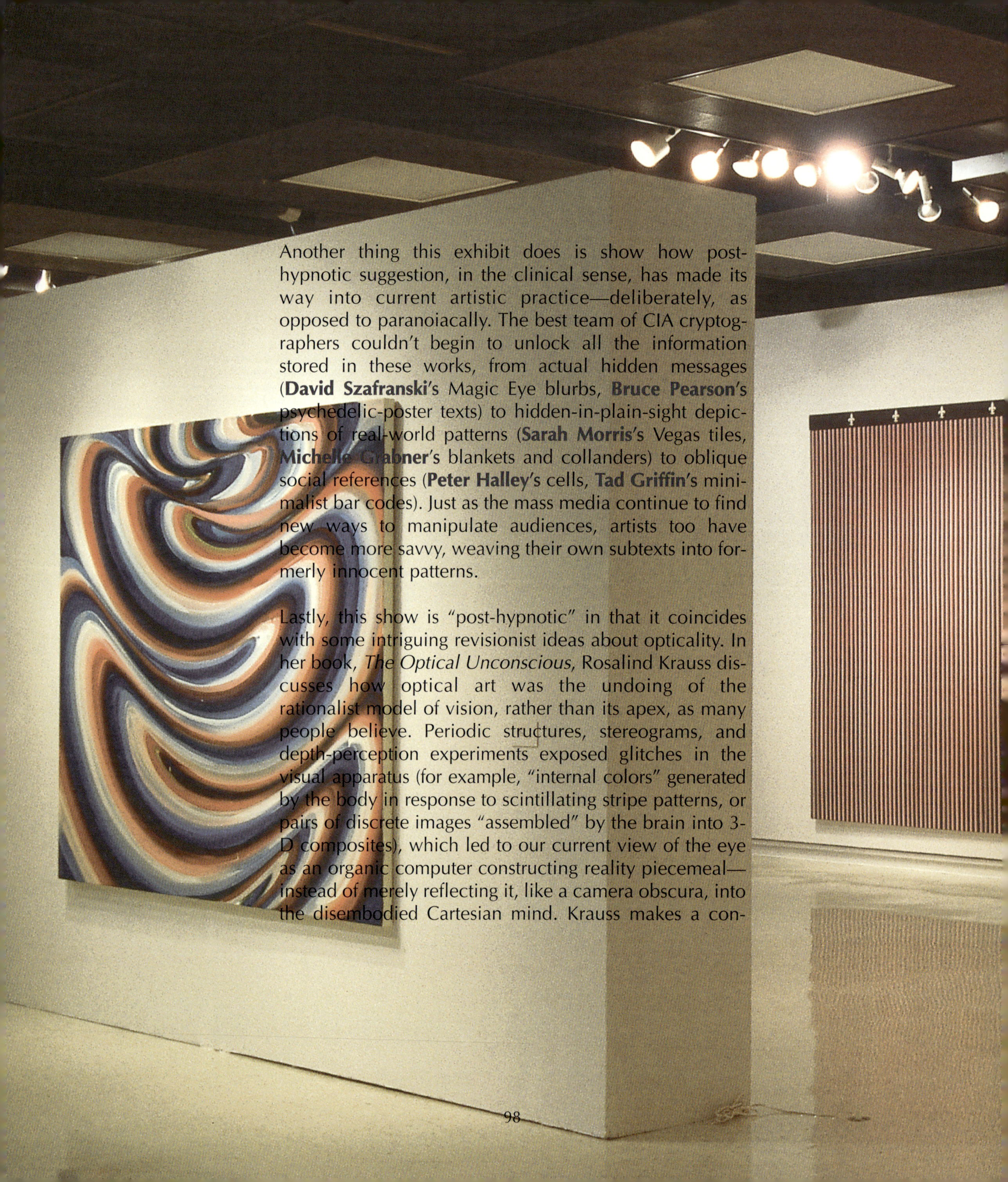

Another thing this exhibit does is show how post-hypnotic suggestion, in the clinical sense, has made its way into current artistic practice—deliberately, as opposed to paranoiacally. The best team of CIA cryptographers couldn't begin to unlock all the information stored in these works, from actual hidden messages (**David Szafranski**'s Magic Eye blurbs, **Bruce Pearson**'s psychedelic-poster texts) to hidden-in-plain-sight depictions of real-world patterns (**Sarah Morris**'s Vegas tiles, **Michelle Grabner**'s blankets and collanders) to oblique social references (**Peter Halley**'s cells, **Tad Griffin**'s minimalist bar codes). Just as the mass media continue to find new ways to manipulate audiences, artists too have become more savvy, weaving their own subtexts into formerly innocent patterns.

Lastly, this show is "post-hypnotic" in that it coincides with some intriguing revisionist ideas about opticality. In her book, *The Optical Unconscious,* Rosalind Krauss discusses how optical art was the undoing of the rationalist model of vision, rather than its apex, as many people believe. Periodic structures, stereograms, and depth-perception experiments exposed glitches in the visual apparatus (for example, "internal colors" generated by the body in response to scintillating stripe patterns, or pairs of discrete images "assembled" by the brain into 3-D composites), which led to our current view of the eye as an organic computer constructing reality piecemeal—instead of merely reflecting it, like a camera obscura, into the disembodied Cartesian mind. Krauss makes a convincing case for the temporality and "carnality" of vision, in contrast to Clement Greenberg's view of it as something instantaneous and cerebral. Much of the work in this show—from **Yayoi Kusama**'s labor-intensive doodling to **Karin Davie**'s muscular brush movements—reminds us that vision takes place in time and is rooted in the physical body.

In the 70s and 80s it became customary to refer to Op art as a "failed movement," a flash in the pan of art history. But considering how many artists continue to return to Op motifs (or how many times the word "Op" appears in newspaper and magazine listings, even as a shorthand reference), "failed" is probably not the right word. Stripped of utopian trappings, the perceptual investigation goes on, and new technology provides new subject matter to be embraced or critiqued. The preceding pictures and statements suggest that Op art—like the monochrome—has as many rationales in the 90s as there are artists doing it. What's "over" is the idea of a monolithic movement based solely on formal, rationalist criteria.

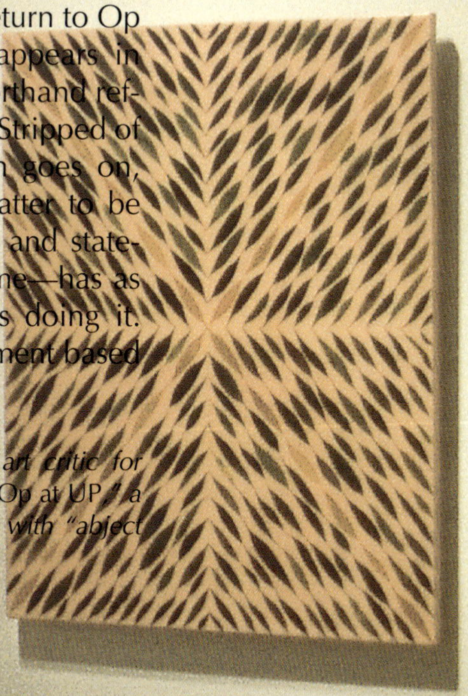

Moody, one of the artists in post-hypnotic, *is also an art critic for* Artforum *and other publications. In 1998, he organized "Op at UP," a five-person exhibition at UP & Co in New York dealing with "abject Op" in the 90s.*

list of works

*denotes works reproduced but not included in the exhibition
bold numbers denote page numbers
dimensions: height precedes width precedes depth

John Armleder
12, 13. GOG Suite, 1996
Silkscreen ink on paper
19 5/8 x 19 5/8 inches
2 prints from a suite of 13, #19 of ed. 25
Courtesy Sollertis Gallery, Toulouse

Ross Bleckner
16.* The Arrangement of Things, 1982
Oil on canvas, 96 x 162 inches
Museum of Fine Arts, Boston. Reproduced with permission. © 1999 Museum of Fine Arts, Boston. All Rights Reserved.
Photo: courtesy Mary Boone Gallery, New York

17. Brothers' Swords, 1986
Oil on canvas, 108 x 84 inches
The Broad Art Foundation, Santa Monica, California
Photo: courtesy Mary Boone Gallery, New York

Stratton Cherouny
18, 19. Untitled #29 and **#34**, 1998
Acrylic polymer and pigment on wood
12 7/8 inches diameter
Courtesy the artist

David Clarkson
22.* Performance-enhanced, 1998
Enamel on wood with lightbulbs
28 x 28 x 2 inches
Courtesy Derek Eller Gallery, New York
Photo: courtesy the artist

23. Iris Seventh Avenue Style, 1998
Enamel on wood with light bulbs
47 inches diameter x 2 inches
Private collection

Mark Dagley
24.* Primary Color Vortex, 1995
Acrylic on canvas, 72 x 72 inches
Courtesy Galerie Bischofberger, Zürich

25. Concentric Sequence, 1996
Acrylic and pencil on canvas, 72 x 72 inches
Courtesy UP & Co, New York

Karin Davie
28. Wanted, 1998
Oil on canvas, 72 x 96 inches
Collection Ernesto Esposito
Courtesy the artist and Marianne Boesky Gallery, New York

29.* Over, 1998
Oil on canvas, 72 x 60 inches
Collection Victoria Love
Photo: courtesy Marianne Boesky Gallery

Steve Di Benedetto
30.* Untitled, 1989
Acrylic on canvas, 30 x 30 inches
Photo: courtesy Tony Shafrazi Gallery, New York

31. Scan, 1989
Acrylic on canvas, 120 x 42 inches
Courtesy Tony Shafrazi Gallery, New York

Michelle Grabner
34. Screen #2 (orange), 1998-99
Enamel on medex, 32 x 34 inches
Courtesy Ten in One Gallery, New York

35.* Fuzzy Blkt #4, 1998
Enamel and flock/medex, 28 x 24 inches
Courtesy Rocket Gallery, London

Tad Griffin
36. Echolate 8, 1994
Oil on canvas, 82 x 72 inches
Courtesy the artist and Texas Gallery, Houston

37.* Untitled L, 1995
Oil on canvas, 72 x 56 inches
Courtesy the artist and Texas Gallery, Houston

Peter Halley
40. Red Cell, 1988
Day-Glo acrylic, Roll-a-Tex on canvas
93 x 108 x 3 inches
The Broad Art Foundation, Santa Monica, California

Peter Halley
41.* A Dangerous Game, 1993
Day-Glo acrylic, and Roll-a-Tex on canvas
84 5/8 x 90 3/4 inches
Collection Mickey Beyer
Photo: courtesy the artist

Jim Isermann
42.* Untitled (fabric wall-hanging), 1993
Pieced cotton and cotton-blend quilt top, 76 x 76 inches
Photo: courtesy Feature Inc., New York

43. Untitled (hole painting), 1987
Enamel on wood, 48 x 48 x 2 inches
Courtesy the artist, Feature Inc., New York, and Richard Telles Fine Art, Los Angeles

Yayoi Kusama
46. Crowd, 1992
Acrylic on canvas, 76 1/4 x 51 3/8 inches
Courtesy Robert Miller Gallery, New York

47.* Dots Accumulation, 1995
Acrylic on canvas, 115 x 90 1/2 inches
Courtesy Robert Miller Gallery, New York

Judy Ledgerwood
48.* Groovin on Lemon & Silver, 1996
Oil and wax on canvas, 84 x 96 inches
Courtesy Feigen Contemporary, New York

49. In the Groove, 1996
Oil and wax on canvas, 84 x 96 inches
Courtesy Feigen Contemporary, New York

Jason Martin
52. Harlot, 1992
Acrylic gel medium on stainless steel
48 x 48 x 1 inches
Courtesy Robert Miller Gallery, New York

53.* Freeway, 1997
Oil on perspex, 47 1/4 x 47 1/4 inches
Collection C.M. Leonard
Photo: courtesy Robert Miller Gallery, New York

Tom Martinelli
54.* Untitled #9626, 1997
Acrylic on canvas, 70 x 76 inches
Courtesy the artist

55. Untitled #9546, 1995
Acrylic on canvas, 76 x 70 inches
Courtesy the artist

Tom Moody
58.* Discs, 1998
Photocopies, linen tape
29 1/2 x 27 inches
Courtesy Derek Eller Gallery, New York

59. Greater, 1997
Photocopies, linen tape
88 x 78 inches
Courtesy Derek Eller Gallery

Sarah Morris
60.* Horizontal Blinds, 1997
Gloss household paint on canvas
84 x 84 inches
Courtesy White Cube, London

61. Bathroom Floor (Las Vegas), 1997
Gloss household paint on canvas,
72 x 72 inches
Collection Arlene B. Richman

Aaron Parazette
64. February, 1997
Oil enamel on canvas, 75 x 75 inches
Collection June W. Mattingly

65.* Horizon Light, 1997
Oil enamel on canvas, 75 x 75 inches
Courtesy the artist and Texas Gallery,
Houston

Bruce Pearson
66.* Die of Pleasure, 1998
Acrylic on styrofoam, 82 x 72 inches
Courtesy Ronald Feldman Fine Arts,
New York

67. Wanna Be Happy Be Happy, 1995
Oil and acrylic on styrofoam,
96 x 71 inches
Collection of Sean Jason Gelb, M.D.

Walter Robinson
70. Green Velvet, 1986
Oil enamel on canvas, 36 x 36 inches
Collection the artist

71. I am Mad, I am Drowning, 1986
Latex and oil enamel on canvas
36 x 36 inches
Collection the artist

Susie Rosmarin
72.* Blue Flash, 1999
Acrylic on canvas, 43 x 37 inches
The Beresford-Ritchie Collection
Courtesy Angstrom Gallery, Dallas

73. Static Study #45, 1998
Acrylic on canvas, 84 x 71 inches
Courtesy the artist and Texas Gallery

Peter Schuyff
76.* Untitled, 1987
Acrylic on linen, 120 x 120 inches
Photo: courtesy Pat Hearn Gallery,
New York

77. Untitled, 1986
Acrylic on linen, 90 x 66 inches
The Broad Art Foundation

Michael Scott
78.* Untitled, 1999
Enamel on aluminum, 33 x 17 inches
Courtesy Sandra Gering Gallery, New York
Photo: courtesy the artist

79. The History of Memory Part 1, 1993
Enamel on aluminum, 78 x 59 inches
Courtesy Sandra Gering Gallery

James Siena
82. Battery, 1997
Enamel on aluminum, 29 x 22 3/4 inches
Collection of Sean Jason Gelb, M.D.
Photo: courtesy Christinerose Gallery,
New York

83. Twirly Three, 1995
Enamel on aluminum, 29 x 22 3/4 inches
Courtesy Christinerose Gallery, New York

David Szafranski
84.* God is in the Details, 1998
Digital ink jet print on paper
Variable dimensions
Courtesy the artist

85. Bra Sale, 1998
Digital ink jet print on paper
Variable dimensions
Courtesy the artist

Philip Taaffe
88.* Big Iris, 1985
Linoprint collage and acrylic on canvas
63 x 63 inches
Courtesy Gagosian Gallery, New York

89. Brest, 1985
Linoprint collage and acrylic on canvas
110 3/4 x 110 3/4 inches
Rubell Family Collection, Miami
Photo: courtesy Gagosian Gallery, New York

Fred Tomaselli
90. Thirteen Thousand, 1992
Aspirin, acrylic, and resin on wood
48 x 47 inches
Collection Jim Kempner

91.* Bird Blast, 1997
Leaves, pills, collage, synthetic polymer
paint and resin on wood
60 x 60 inches
Museum of Modern Art, New York
Gift of Douglas S. Cramer

Yek
94.* Freefalling Farewell, 1999
Acrylic and latex on wood
30 x 30 x 3 inches
Collection David Reed
Photo: courtesy the artist

95. Madness Comes Quickly, 1998
Acrylic and latex on wood
48 x 48 x 7 inches
Courtesy Angstrom Gallery, Dallas

additional works
list of lenders

The following were exhibited only at University Galleries, and are not individually reproduced in the catalogue:

John Armleder
GOG Suite, 1996
silkscreen ink on paper
19 5/8 x 19 5/8 inches
4 prints from a suite of 13, #19 of ed. 25
Courtesy Sollertis Gallery, Toulouse

Stratton Cherouny
Untitled #20, **#24**, **#25**, **#30**, **#31**, **#32**, **#33**, all 1998
acrylic polymer and pigment on wood
12 7/8 inches diameter
Courtesy the artist

David Clarkson
Afterimage Painting (orange), 1998
(included in installation shot, p. 97)
enamel in wood with light bulbs
47 inches diameter x 2 inches
Private collection

Michelle Grabner
Screen #1 (yellow), 1998-99
enamel on medex
32 x 34 inches
Courtesy Ten in One Gallery, New York

Screen #3 (beige), 1998-99
enamel on medex
32 x 34 inches
Courtesy Ten in One Gallery, New York

Walter Robinson
Privileged Domain, 1986
latex and oil enamel on canvas
36 x 36 inches
Collection the artist

The Heat of the Climate, 1986
latex and oil enamel on canvas
36 x 36 inches
Collection the artist

Vacation from the Self, 1986
latex and oil enamel on canvas
36 x 36 inches
Collection the artist

An Ugly Trap, 1986
oil enamel on canvas
36 x 36 inches
Collection Harry Druzd

Fred Tomaselli
X Will Fade, 1992
(included in installation shot, p. 99)
hemp leaves, acrylic and resin on wood panel
32 x 34 inches
Collection Laura Miller, courtesy Christopher Grimes Gallery, Santa Monica

lenders to the exhibition

The Beresford-Ritchie Collection
Marianne Boesky Gallery, New York
Stratton Cherouny
Christinerose Gallery, New York
David Clarkson
Mark Dagley
The Broad Art Foundation, Santa Monica
Derek Eller Gallery, New York
Harry Druzd
Ernesto Esposito
Feature Inc., New York
Feigen Contemporary, New York
Ronald Feldman Fine Arts, New York
Sean Jason Gelb, M.D.
Tad Griffin
Jim Isermann
Jim Kempner
Tom Martinelli
Tom Moody
June W. Mattingly
Laura Miller
Robert Miller Gallery, New York
Museum of Modern Art, New York
Aaron Parazette
Private collections
David Reed
Arlene B. Richman
Walter Robinson
Susie Rosmarin
Rubell Family Collection, Miami
Michael Scott
Tony Shafrazi Gallery, New York
Sollertis Gallery, Toulouse
David Szafranski
Ten in One Gallery, New York
Texas Gallery, Houston
Fred Tomaselli
UP & Co, New York
White Cube, London
Yek

photography credits by page

Brian Albert: 30-32
Ron Amtutz: 81-83
Ted Diamond: 18-19, 34, 43, 61, 64, 67, 70-71, 77, 79, 90, 95
Beth Phillips: front cover, 1, 24
Karl Rademacher: 51, 96-100.
Steven Sloman: 41
Stephen White: 60
Zindman/Fremont: 16, 66-68

selected readings

essays and articles

Diehl, Carol. "Tom Martinelli: Dot, Dot, Dot." *ARTnews,* May 1995, 113.

Heiser, Jorg. "Planetary Folklore: on the Legacy of Victor Vasarely." *frieze.* June-July-August 1998, 62-67.

Horsham, Michael. "Dot Gain: On the Meaning of the Dot." *frieze.* June-July-August 1998, 74-77.

McCormick, Carlo. "pOPTOMETRY." *Artforum.* November 1985, 87-91.

Perrone, Jeff. "Fashion is the Real Thing in Abstraction." *Arts,* Summer 1987, 81-83.

Sharp, Willoughby. "Luminism and Kineticism." *Minimal Art: A Critical Anthology,* edited by Gregory Battcock. New York: E.P. Dutton, 1968, 317-358.

Solomon, Andrew. "Yayoi Kusama: Dot Dot Dot." *Artforum.* February 1997, 66-73, 100, 104, 109. (cover)

Taaffe, Philip. "Sublimity, Now and Forever, Amen." *Arts.* March 1986, 18-19.

Yood, James. "post-hypnotic." *Artforum.* April 1999, 120.

exhibition catalogues

Abstract Painting, Once Removed. Essays by Dana Friis-Hansen, David Pagel, Raphael Rubenstein, and Peter Schjeldahl. Houston, Texas: Contemporary Arts Museum, 1998.

Analogs of Modernism. Essay by Tom Moody. Dallas: Dallas Artists Research and Exhibition, 1995.

Ross Bleckner. Essays by Lisa Dennison, Thomas Crow, and Simon Watney. New York: Guggenheim Museum, 1995.

David Clarkson: Highlight Paintings. Essays by Bill Arning, Deborah Esch, and Saul Ostrow. New York: White Columns, 1992.

Karin Davie: Odalisques. Essay by Barry Schwabsky. Los Angeles: Kim Light Gallery and Jason Rubell Gallery, 1993.

Cold Days: Judy Ledgerwood. Essay by Craig Adcock. Chicago: The Renaissance Society at the University of Chicago, 1999.

Contemporary Perspectives 1: Abstraction in Question. Essays by Bruce Ferguson, Joan Simon, and Roberta Smith. Sarasota, Florida: The John and Mable Ringling Museum of Art, 1989.

Fifteen: Jim Isermann Survey. Essays by David Pagel and Michael Darling. The Institute of Visual Arts, University of Wisconsin-Milwaukee, 1998.

Michelle Grabner: Home Painting. Interview by Jérôme Sans. Oxfordshire: The Rocket Press, 1998.

Peter Halley: Paintings 1989-92. Essays by Dan Cameron, Michael Danoff, and Deborah Leviton. Des Moines: The Des Moines Art Center, 1993.

Hines & His Circle: Tragic Fading Supergraphic. Houston: Art of This Century, 1996.

Jason Martin: Paintings. Essay by Mark Gisbourne. London: Lisson Gallery, 1998.

Sarah Morris: Modern Worlds. Essays by Michael Bracewell and Jan Winkelmann. Interview by Michael Tarantino. Oxford: Museum of Modern Art, 1999.

Post-Abstract Abstraction. Essay by Eugene Schwartz. Ridgefield, Connecticut: The Aldrich Museum of Contemporary Art, 1987.

Post-Pop, Post-Pictures. Essay by Courtenay Smith. Chicago: The David and Alfred Smart Museum of Art, The University of Chicago, 1997.

Projects 63: Karin Davie, Udomsak Krisanamis, Bruce Pearson, Fred Tomaselli. Pamphlet. Essay by Lilian Tone and Anne Umland. New York: Museum of Modern Art, 1998.

Bridget Riley: Paintings from the 1960s and 70s. Essays by Lisa G. Corrin, Robert Kudielka, and Frances Spalding. London: Serpentine Gallery, 1999.

Michael Scott: New Paintings. Essay by Robert Nickas. New York: Tony Shafrazi Gallery, 1990.

James Siena. Essay by Geoffrey Young. New York: Cristinerose Gallery, 1997.

Static. Essays by Tom Moody and John Pomara and Alexander Ross. New York: Eugene Binder, 1998.

Fred Tomaselli. Essays by Alisa Tager and David A. Greene. Santa Monica, California: Christopher Grimes Gallery, 1995.

Fred Tomaselli. Interview with Fred Tomaselli by James Rondeau. Berlin: Galerie Gebauer, 1999.

The Void Each Time: Steve Di Benedetto, Shirley Kaneda, and Michael Scott. Essays by Demetrio Paparoni, David Pagel, and Robert Nickas. Torino, Italy: Edzioni Galleria In Arco, 1992.

Ultra Buzz: Karin Davie, Peter Hopkins, Tom Moody, James Siena, Fred Tomaselli. Pamphlet. Essay by Barry Blinderman. Overland Park, Kansas: Johnson County Community College Gallery of Art, 1999.

Vasarely. Text by Werner Spies. New York: Harry N. Abrams Inc., 1969.

Yayoi Kusama: Now. Essay by Damien Hirst. New York: Robert Miller Gallery, 1998.

Yayoi Kusama: A Retrospective. Essays by Bhupendra Karia and Alexandra Munroe. New York: Center for International Contemporary Arts, 1989.

books

Barrett, Cyril. *Op Art.* New York: Viking, 1970.

Dennett, Daniel C., *Consciousness Explained.* Little Brown and Company, Boston, 1991.

Gombrich, E. H., *The Sense of Order.* London: Phaidon Press Ltd., 1984.

Halley, Peter. *Collected Essays: 1981-87.* Zurich: Bruno Bischofberger Gallery, 1988.

Hickey, Dave. *Air Guitar: Essays on Art & Democracy.* Los Angeles: Art Issues. Press, 1997.

Kandinsky, Wassily. *On the Spiritual in Art.* Edited by Hilla Rebay. New York: The Solomon R. Guggenheim Foundation, 1946.

Kudielka, Robert, ed. *Bridget Riley: Dialogues on Art.* London: Zwemmer, 1995.

Madeleine-Perdrillat, Alain. *Seurat.* New York: Rizzoli International Publications, Inc., 1990.

McLuhan, Marshall. *Understanding Media,* with an introduction by Lewis H. Lapham. Cambridge: MIT Press, 1964.

Seitz, William C. *The Responsive Eye.* New York: Museum of Modern Art, 1965.

acknowledgements

I am deeply indebted to the following artists, collectors, museums, foundations, galleries, and individuals, who generously shared information, insights, technical assistance, artwork, and photographic materials: Greg Bowen, Richard Bruce at Robert Miller Gallery, Stratton Cherouny, David Clarkson, Mark Dagley, Karin Davie, Derek Eller Gallery, Brice Fauché at Sollertis Galerie, Raymond Foye, Sharon Helgason Gallagher and Avery Lozada at D.A.P., Dana Friis-Hansen at the Contemporary Arts Museum in Houston, Michelle Grabner, Juliana Hanner at the Broad Art Foundation, Peter Halley, Dave Hickey, George Horner at Tony Shafrazi Gallery, Fredericka Hunter at Texas Gallery, Dan Iwaszco and Roberta Merryman at Bolger, Julie Kirkpatrick at Marianne Boesky Gallery, Dave Kuntz, Douglas Lamb, Sheldon La Pierre, Judy Ledgerwood, Joel Leib at Ten in One Gallery, Tom Martinelli, Robert McKeever at Gagosian Gallery, Ron Mottram, I.S.U. Art Department Chair, the Museum of Modern Art, Aaron Parazette, Mariacristina Parravicini at Cristinerose Gallery, Bruce Pearson, Jim Pedersen and Hudson at Feature, Uscha Pohl at UP & CO, Tim Porges, Daniel Reich at Pat Hearn Gallery, Walter Robinson, Susie Rosmarin, Don Rubell, John Runyon at Turner & Runyon Gallery, Michael Scott, Courtenay Smith, David Szafranski, Fred Tomaselli, Ron Warren at Mary Boone Gallery, and Yek.

I would also like to express appreciation to my colleagues at the museums participating in post-hypnotic's tour: Theresa Jones and Mary Nicolett at The MAC; David Brown, Rachael Vaters-Carr, Lisa Buck, Michelle Padilla, and Kim Humphries at The Contemporary Arts Center; Chris Scoates and Karen Beall at the Atlanta College of Art Gallery; Gregory Knight and Edward Maldanado at the Chicago Cultural Center; and Peter Spooner at the Tweed Musuem of Art. Thank you for your enthusiasm, advice, and help in organizing and maintaining the travel of the exhibition.

The National Endowment for the Arts and the Illinois Arts Council provided funds without which post-hypnotic could not have developed beyond the dreaming stages.

My staff at University Galleries has worked creatively and diligently throughout the planning and realization of this publication and exhibition: Angela Barker, Registrar, deftly handled the myriad details involving loans, insurance, shipping, scheduling, receptions, and general communications. Matt Pulford, Assistant to the Director, ably compiled text and reproductions, and also assisted in book and installation design. Preparator Karl Rademacher designed crates for the tour, advised the installation crew in Dallas, and has worked wonders improving our facility. Gallery assistants Stacey Yeakel and Kelly Donovan transcribed tapes and offered design input. Curator Bill Conger tirelessly planned, scanned, co-designed, compiled, and reformatted this publication—without him, the book would possibly have been finished in the next millenium.

Tom Moody has been my collaborator and co-conspirator since nearly the beginning of post-hypnotic. His wit, creative input, and remarkable editing of texts has been essential to the project's success.

Finally, thanks to my dearest Laura Edwards for her patience, French translations, and proofing assistance.

Barry Blinderman
Director of University Galleries

ILLINOIS STATE
UNIVERSITY